AF815534

#1 BESTSELLER

Charting Your RETIREMENT JOURNEY

A ROADMAP TO CREATE MEANING, JOY, AND PURPOSE IN YOUR NEW CHAPTER

FREE BONUS DOWNLOAD THE WORKSHEETS

JOHN ELBING & LUISA COLOMBO

Flash the QR code

and download all the worksheets.

THIS BOOK IS FOR YOU IF YOU ARE

- Approaching retirement and wondering, what's next?
- Recently retired and not ready to "just slow down"
- Feeling stuck in a routine and craving new purpose
- Curious about exploring possibilities you've never dared before
- Someone who has always put others first and is ready to design life on your own terms
- Eager to make the next chapter of your life meaningful, creative, and fun
- Open to experimenting, prototyping, and playing your way into new futures
- Looking for practical tools to imagine, test, and build your best life yet

BECAUSE YOU WILL

- Discover who you really are today — what energizes you, what drains you, and what matters most
- Unlock bold new possibilities for your future, from practical to wildly adventurous
- Learn how to prototype your life and "test drive" ideas before committing
- Gain clarity and confidence in your decision-making
- Shift to an agile, joyful mindset that embraces exploration over perfection
- Build the habits and tools to design a purposeful, fulfilling life after 55, 60, or 65

Charting Your Retirement Journey

© 2025 John Elbing & Luisa Columbo

All Rights Reserved. No part of this book may be reproduced, distributed, or transmitted in any form or by any means, including photocopying, recording, or other electronic or mechanical methods, without the prior written permission of the publisher, except in the case of brief quotations in reviews.

Publishing:

Epic Author Publishing

support@epicauthor.com - www.epicauthor.com

Illustrations:
By Luisa Colombo

Cover design, and layout:
By tucity tucitydesign@gmail.com

ISBNs:

Paperback: 978-1-947276-82-6

eBook: 978-1-947276-81-9

First Edition: December 2025

For bulk orders, interviews, or speaking engagements, visit:
chartingyourretirementjourney.com

Printed all over the world.

Luisa and I met through a shared curiosity about using design thinking to shape a meaningful life. That path led to this book, but, more importantly, to our close friendship. So...

To this book project. To Luisa.

To my exceptional daughter, for whom I am trying to be a decent role model.

To my wonderful partner, who brightens my life.

And to my fluffy cat.

JOHN ELBING

To John, whose curiosity, kindness, humor, and creative mind made this journey deeper, lighter, and more meaningful—and whose friendship is the gift I cherish most.

To my husband, whose presence is both my anchor and my joy.

To my sons, who show me every day what it means to grow with curiosity, courage and heart.

LUISA COLOMBO

TABLE OF CONTENTS

01
Preface

You've worked hard. Built a career. Collected the wins (and maybe a few scars). Now retirement is close enough to see on the calendar. And yet, instead of a champagne countdown, there's this... itch.

You can't quite name it, but it sounds like:

> *"Spending retirement doing macramé would drive me crazy."*
>
> *"Hitting the quarterly sales quota just doesn't thrill me anymore."*
>
> *"Money's fine, but it's not filling the gap."*
>
> *"Work and family used to be my whole world—where did my passions wander off to?"*
>
> *"I could be helping people in ways that go beyond writing checks."*

If any of that feels familiar, congratulations, you're human. And you're standing at the best crossroads of your life.

This is the moment to stop, breathe, and actually look around. To take stock, not just of what you've done, but of what's still possible. The goal of this book is simple: to help you choose a life you'll love waking up to, one that keeps you lit up well into the decades ahead.

You picked up this book because you feel that nudge. That whisper. That restlessness. Good. That's your invitation to explore new paths.
So... What now?

We're going to walk this road together. Through questions, exercises, and a little bit of self-prodding, you'll start peeling away the blinders. You'll find the parts of yourself you've been missing. You'll learn what really drives you, and how to aim that energy in directions that make you happy.

It starts simply: grab a notebook and your favorite pen, pour yourself a coffee (or tea, or something sparkly), and open your mind.

Step by step, you'll:

- Trade "stuck" for "in motion."
- Swap ruts for fresh tracks.
- Expand your horizon until you can see possibilities you never noticed before.
- Feel the freedom to build a life that feels yours again.

This isn't about filling time. It's about filling your life.

Let's get started.

02
Introduction

WHO IS THIS FOR?

You're closing in on 60. Your career is solid. You've climbed the ladder, collected the wins, and ticked plenty of boxes.

And yet… something's off.

Retirement pops into your head more often now—sometimes as a daydream, sometimes as a question mark. Maybe that's part of the unease.

When we talk to people like you, we hear things like:

> *"Retirement used to be a postcard dream. Now it feels like a storm cloud on the horizon."*
>
> *"When I picture my days after I stop working, all I see is endless time to fill—and pottery won't save me from the boredom."*
>
> *"I've been grinding for decades. But for what, exactly?"*
>
> *"Promotions and pay raises used to light a fire in me. Now they feel like empty trophies. Was it all worth it?"*
>
> *"I spent my life chained to the job. No time to give back. Lately, the urge to help others won't leave me alone."*
>
> *"Maybe it's sudden, maybe it's been creeping in for years—but my work feels paper-thin. Now I get what people mean when they talk about 'meaning.'"*
>
> *"Retirement? It's starting to look less like freedom and more like a slow fade. I'm not ready to disappear."*
>
> *"I've started taking inventory of my career—and my life. What's on the list that truly matters?"*
>
> *"I worked for my family. Now the kids are grown, and the house feels too quiet."*
>
> *"The calendar says I'm nearing retirement, but I've still got gas in the tank. How do you keep contributing in a world that treats anyone over 50 like a fossil?"*

If that sounds like your inner voice, then yes, this is for you.

Some people can't wait to clock out for good—slow mornings, long lunches, hobbies that have been on the back burner for decades. And that's fine.

Others? Not so much.

Lately, the buzz is all about the younger crowd—Gen Z, younger millennials—who seem to treat work less like a life sentence and more like a tool. They chase purpose over titles, embrace change without apology, and insist on flexibility so they can actually *live* while they work.

Is all of that true? Maybe, maybe not. But there's something about the attitude that's worth stealing.

Thirty years ago, the rules were different. Career was king. Loyalty was a badge of honor. Duty was the default setting.

But now? Now you get to rewrite the rules for yourself. Maybe it's time to put purpose ahead of career. To trade blind loyalty for intentional change. To swap rigid duty for flexibility that lets you thrive.

The so-called "retirement age" isn't a wall you slam into—it's a door you can choose to open in any direction.

So, here's the real question: **What do you want from the rest of your life—and what's stopping you from starting now?**

WHY NOW?

They say the best time to start was twenty years ago. The second-best? **Right now**.

There's no better moment to choose a life that actually makes you happy. Not "someday." Not "after things calm down." Not "once I retire."

Right now, you still have the one resource you can never get back once it's gone: time. Time to explore. Time to experiment. Time to try things on for size, to fail fast, to discover what lights you up, and to start building toward it.

That's what we're here for—to guide you through it, step by step.

The clock is ticking, but that's not bad news. It's your cue.

WHY THIS BOOK?

We are Luisa and John.

We've been where you are, staring at the road ahead, wondering if we're on the right one, second-guessing the turns we've taken. We've zigged. We've zagged. We've had moments of doubt so strong they could've been full-time jobs.

And here's what we've learned: the zigs and zags aren't detours—they're the point. The journey matters more than the destination.

Somewhere along the way, we each found a path that felt right—impactful, flexible, and open-ended enough to keep us curious. And now, we want to help you find yours.

Luisa spent her career in human resources, leadership, and career coaching before becoming an independent consultant. She blends everything she's learned with agile practices to help organizations rethink not just how they work—but how they think about work.

John's worn a lot of hats—software engineer, project manager, change manager, digital marketer, startup founder. He used to change jobs every couple of years out of boredom. Now he changes roles every couple of hours—coaching startups, facilitating workshops, teaching, mentoring, building stories, and, most importantly, always learning.

Between us, we've trained in countless techniques—some personal, some project-focused—all rooted in understanding people. We've handpicked the exercises that pack the biggest punch, the ones that help our clients break out of ruts and into possibilities.

This book comes from years of running an online course on reinvention—especially during the pandemic—and adapting it with real feedback from people just like you. Except now, it's even more focused on your stage of life, your opportunities, your challenges.

Our mission? Simple:

Stop…

- Feeling stuck.
- Worrying about your future.
- Seeing retirement as a slow fade-out.
- Moving forward without purpose.
- Waiting for "someday."

Start…

- Feeling confident about what's next.
- Looking forward to your next chapter.
- Finding meaning in your work.
- Feeling fulfilled in your life.
- Choosing what matters to you.

We're here to help you design the next 20 years you'll be proud of. And when that's done? We'll check in for the next 20.

READY FOR A CHANGE

Change starts the moment you decide you're done standing still.

Before we go any further, ask yourself: are you truly ready? Ready to break routines, ditch "someday," and reach for something that matters?

If the answer is yes, let's begin.

ACCEPT

First, let's get honest.

Are you willing to accept that…

- You may have been blessed with more opportunities than most.
- You've likely achieved plenty—both in your career and in your personal life.
- You have every reason to feel grateful for it all.

And yet... there's this whisper. Something's missing. Something doesn't fit anymore. You're uneasy about what's next.

If you can admit that—and if you're ready to do something about it—you've already taken the first real step toward change.

Acceptance isn't about giving up. It's about opening your eyes to the gap between "what is" and "what could be." That's the fuel for everything that comes next.

But before you leap into action, you need to know exactly where you're standing now. Otherwise, you risk chasing the wrong solution—something that looks great on paper but doesn't make you any happier in real life.

This is your life. There's no one-size-fits-all fix. You are unique. Your answers should be, too.

That's why we start with a set of exercises designed to help you see your life clearly as it is today. There are no right or wrong answers, only answers that are true for *you.*

Tips for this stage:

- **Be brutally honest.** Don't waste time building a life that isn't yours.
- **Don't overthink.** Your first instinct is usually the most revealing.
- **Drop the guilt.** Forget "By now I should know..." Instead, remember: *I am where I need to be, and I know what I know.*

This might take a while—but it's worth it. You're not just passing the time. You're building the rest of your life.

2.1 MEET ALEX

We didn't want this book to be just theory. We wanted it to feel lived-in—tested by people with real hopes, real worries, and real lives in motion.

That's where our beta readers came in. We had the privilege of working with several amazing people who read early drafts, tried the exercises, and told us—honestly—what worked, what didn't, and what needed rethinking.

***Alex** is one of them.*

Alex isn't a made-up case study. They're a real person who walked through this process while we were writing it—reading, reflecting, and sharing unfiltered feedback. Sometimes they said, "This part really clicked." Sometimes they said, "Nope, this isn't landing." And sometimes they gave us the kind of pause-and-think insight that made us rewrite entire sections.

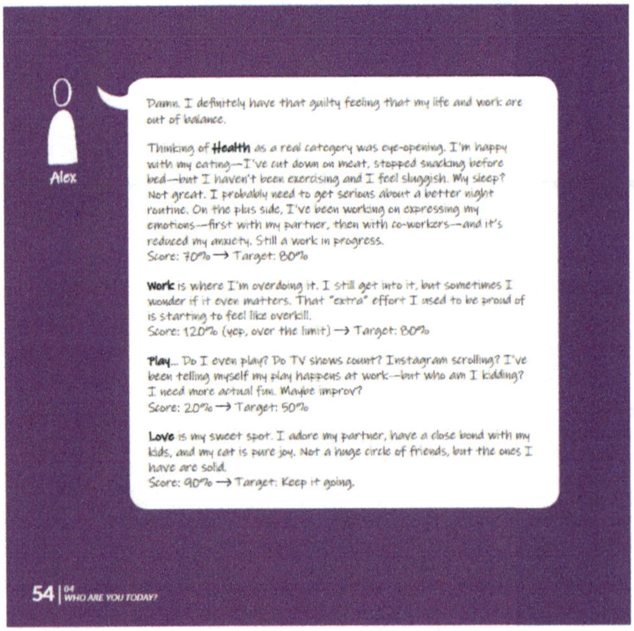
Alex

Damn. I definitely have that guilty feeling that my life and work are out of balance.

Thinking of **Health** as a real category was eye-opening. I'm happy with my eating—I've cut down on meat, stopped snacking before bed—but I haven't been exercising and I feel sluggish. My sleep? Not great. I probably need to get serious about a better night routine. On the plus side, I've been working on expressing my emotions—first with my partner, then with co-workers—and it's reduced my anxiety. Still a work in progress.
Score: 70% → Target: 80%

Work is where I'm overdoing it. I still get into it, but sometimes I wonder if it even matters. That "extra" effort I used to be proud of is starting to feel like overkill.
Score: 120% (yep, over the limit) → Target: 80%

Play... Do I even play? Do TV shows count? Instagram scrolling? I've been telling myself my play happens at work—but who am I kidding? I need more actual fun. Maybe improv?
Score: 20% → Target: 50%

Love is my sweet spot. I adore my partner, have a close bond with my kids, and my cat is pure joy. Not a huge circle of friends, but the ones I have are solid.
Score: 90% → Target: Keep it going.

54 | 04 WHO ARE YOU TODAY?

*Throughout the book, you'll find **Alex Boxes**—snapshots of their journey. You'll see when they wrestled with tough questions, when they had "aha" moments, and when they admitted they were stuck. Alex's story isn't perfectly smooth, and that's exactly why it's valuable—it's real.*

Alex is just one voice among many who helped shape this book, but we chose to highlight them because their journey captures the spirit of what this process is all about: being willing to look closely, think deeply, and take steps toward a life that truly fits.

We hope that as you follow along, Alex's experiences will help you feel less alone, more understood, and more inspired to keep going—especially on the days when change feels big and uncertain.

So, thank you, Alex. And thank you to all our beta readers. For your honesty. For your curiosity. For letting us share pieces of your journeys so that others, like you, can build a life they love.

John & Luisa

03

Overview

3.1 WE ARE PROPOSING A JOURNEY. WHAT WILL IT LOOK LIKE?

We've built a step-by-step process for you—a series of exercises designed to take you from **Where am I now?** to **This is the life I want**. All you need is honesty, a willingness to change, and an open mind for new ideas and options. Follow our lead, and you'll be amazed where you end up.

WHO ARE YOU TODAY?

We'll start at the core: you.

You'll ask yourself questions you may not have touched in years—maybe ever. This is where you'll clarify your view of yourself and plant the first flag in your new journey.

You'll move beyond the old "work/life balance" cliché and take a real inventory of who you are and how you operate:

- Refresh your self-image with a personality test.
- Check whether your work and life values are in sync.
- Uncover your deepest motivations.
- Track what excites you and fuels your energy.
- Explore the kinds of work cultures where you thrive.
- Take stock of your skills and competencies.

This is the foundation for everything else. Build it strong.

WHAT IS IMPORTANT TO YOU?

Here's where we reframe your situation and define your *real* "problem."

What do you truly want? What's in your control—and what isn't? You'll learn tools to define, reframe, and explore your challenges so you can design better solutions.

We'll help you take off the blinders, question your usual story, and prepare to see possibilities you didn't know were there.

YOU HAVE MORE POSSIBILITIES THAN YOU THINK

From the comfortable and predictable to the bold and wild—you'll imagine futures across the spectrum.

You'll explore opportunities tied to your skills, dream up inspiring futures, and design several very different Adventures. Yes—this includes daring to consider the "impossible" ones.

ROLE-PLAY YOUR FUTURE LIFE

You'll take these options for a test drive. What would they actually feel like?

We'll walk you through:

- Considering your "stakeholders" (the people affected by your plan).
- Crafting your "value proposition."
- Learning how to talk about your plans and get useful feedback.
- Evaluating risks and spotting dealbreakers early.

This step adds depth—and reality—to your vision.

HOW DO YOU KNOW IF YOU SHOULD JUMP?

Even when you're excited, committing can feel like stepping off a cliff.

We'll help you take a step back, look objectively at each part of your project, and be more systematic in your decision-making. You'll adopt an agile mindset—breaking big leaps into smaller, lower-risk steps—and organize your tasks so progress feels steady and achievable.

By the end, you'll be ready to decide.

THIS IS YOUR PATH

This book isn't about handing you *our* solution—it's about giving you the tools to create *yours*.

And no two paths will look the same.

EXERCISES, WORKSHEETS, AND GETTING ORGANIZED

A journey like this deserves a little structure.

The exercises build on each other, so you'll want to revisit earlier answers, refine them, and see how your thinking evolves. Keep your work together—whether in a printed workbook (flash the **QR code** to download all the worksheets from our companion site "**CraftingYourRetirementJourney.com**"), a notebook, a sketchbook, poster-sized sheets, or even audio or video recordings.

Do it your way. But do it.

P. S. Doing these exercises only in your head doesn't count. That's like going to the gym, watching everyone else work out, and expecting your muscles to grow.

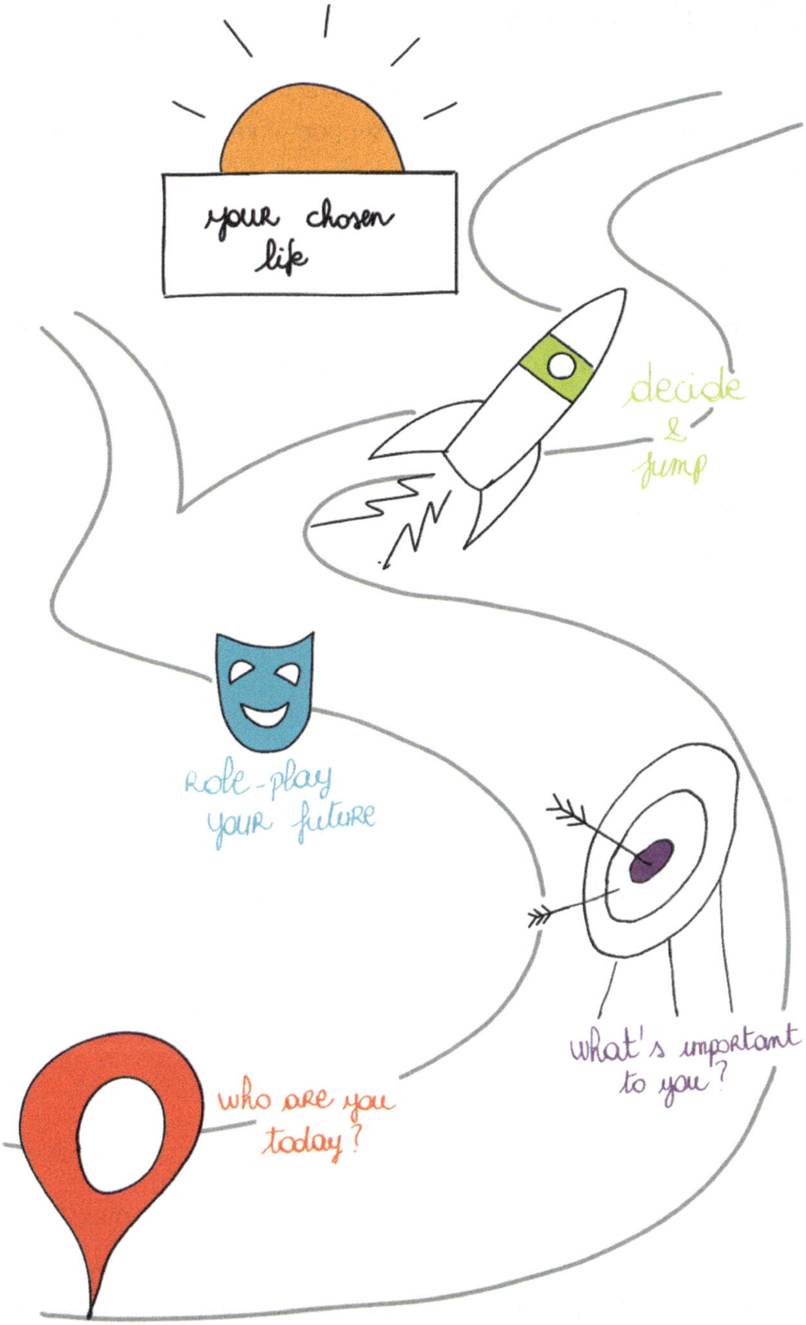
your chosen life
decide & jump
role-play your future
What's important to you?
who are you today?

3.2 CONNECTIONS

You don't have to navigate this journey alone. In fact, you'll go further—and enjoy it more—if you surround yourself with people who inspire, support, and challenge you. Here's how to start building (or rebuilding) those connections.

BEGIN WITH WHAT YOU'VE GOT

Before chasing new contacts, look at your current circle. Think about the communities you're already part of—at work, in your neighborhood, in hobby groups, or online forums. You might be surprised how many potential allies you already know.

SHOW UP WHERE THE ACTION IS

Conferences. Meetups. Workshops. Community events. There's no shortage of gatherings where you can meet people who share your interests or curiosity. You don't have to speak, present, or sell anything—just attend, listen, and let conversations happen naturally.

FOLLOW THE SPARKS

Online, find thought leaders and curious minds who are exploring topics you care about. Read their work, comment thoughtfully, ask questions. Use the internet like a detective—follow the trails of interesting ideas until you discover new voices and fresh perspectives.

PRACTICE THE ART OF GRATITUDE

One of the fastest ways to deepen a connection? Say thank you. Not the generic "Thanks!" but a specific, personal note of appreciation.

Here's your challenge:

1. **Private thanks** – Choose one person to thank in a personal message. Tell them exactly what they did for you, when, and why it mattered.
2. **Public thanks** – Choose another person to thank openly—on LinkedIn, Twitter, a community forum, or even your company's intranet. Shine a light on them in front of others.

Both will make someone's day. And both will make you feel good, too.

Expanding your network isn't about collecting business cards—it's about collecting genuine connections. Approach it with curiosity, generosity, and a willingness to keep showing up. The rest will follow.

When I got to this section, I figured, **why not?** I decided to reach out to a former colleague who, years ago, had taken a chance on me with a project way outside my comfort zone.

I sent a quick message:

"Hey, I was thinking about that project we worked on in 2014. You took a risk on me, and it completely changed how I saw myself. Just wanted you to know I still appreciate it—big time."

I wasn't expecting much. Maybe a polite "thanks." Instead, I got a reply within the hour—warm, surprised, and full of "what are you up to these days?"

By the end of the week, we were already talking about collaborating on a brand-new initiative together.

Here's the thing: it wasn't about **getting** anything out of it. The real win was remembering that I already have amazing people in my corner. The fact it turned into a new opportunity? Total cherry on top.

Alex

Let's get started.

YOU ARE HERE
YOU ARE HERE
YOU ARE HERE

04

Who are you today?

Before you design your future, you need a clear picture of the present. In this chapter, you'll take stock of your health, work, play, and love, explore your personality and motivations, and create a snapshot of who you really are right now. This self-portrait becomes the foundation for everything that follows.

Before you can design your next chapter, you need to know exactly who's starring in it: you.

In this chapter, you'll trade vague notions of "work/life balance" for a deeper, richer picture of your life right now. You'll explore four key areas—**health, work, play, and love**—to see how they fit together (or don't).

You will:

- Take a personality test to uncover your natural traits and hidden motivations.
- Track what fuels your energy—and what drains it.
- Map your work history to spot the cultures where you truly thrive.

And then? You'll gather these discoveries into a personal collage—a visual snapshot of the many sides of you. By the end, you won't just know yourself better; you'll have a clear, grounded foundation for shaping the future you actually want.

WHY THE QUESTION?

Imagine you're planning the ultimate road trip. Before you pick the route, you'd ask yourself: How do I like to travel—fast and direct, or slow and scenic? Do I want to explore museums, mountains, or music festivals? Is the thrill in the arrival… or in everything along the way?

And before all that—you'd start with the map. *Where am I right now? Where have I been before? What parts did I love? What would I skip next time? What was comfortable, what was exciting, and what was missing?*

Now swap "road trip" for "life." You're about to plan your next chapter.

So, **who are you today?**

You're not the same person you were 20 years ago (even if you've been carrying around the same mental snapshot). Some questions you haven't asked yourself in ages. Some answers may surprise you.

Knowing who you are right now is the key to making smart choices about where to go next. This is your chance to update your self-portrait—kindly, honestly, and with fresh eyes.

Great question… though a little scary. How do I even begin to answer it? A few exercises might help me see things more clearly.

Sure, I think I know who I am—I've known my likes and dislikes for years. But maybe there's more under the surface.

Let's find out. Nothing to lose… and maybe a few surprises to gain.

Alex

4.1 HOW ARE YOU GOING TO DO THIS?

Ever stood in front of one of those triple mirrors in a fitting room? Suddenly you're seeing yourself from angles you never normally notice. That's exactly what we're going to do here—except instead of your outfit, we're looking at your life.

You'll examine yourself from multiple perspectives, using different tools and exercises to get a complete, multi-faceted view. Each activity will zoom in on one aspect—your life, your personality, your preferences. Then you'll step back, reflect, and note the patterns, surprises, and questions that surface.

By the end, you'll have built a **collage of you**—a snapshot that captures all the sides you've just uncovered.

We'll start with an inventory of your life and work, plus a simple personality test. Think of it as the "front view" in that mirror—familiar, comfortable. It will also nudge you into an introspective mindset, because from here on out, it's all about you.

Next, you'll explore the other angles: describing different areas of your life in detail. Along the way, you may notice places where a tweak—or a big change—could make things better.

By the time we're done, you won't just see yourself more clearly. You'll understand yourself more deeply.

THE EXERCISES

Here we go. There's only one real way to learn more about yourself—**you have to do the work**.

The exercises we've gathered here are designed to make you more aware of where you stand today: your preferences, patterns, and the lessons you've picked up along your path so far. Some will feel familiar. Others may surprise you. All of them will give you pieces of the puzzle.

The exercises in a nutshell:

BASE CAMP CHECK-IN

Forget the tired "work/life balance" equation. You'll explore four essential dimensions—**health, work, play, and love**—and see if you've got the right dose of each.

EXPLORER'S PROFILE

Traits don't define you, but they shape how you see the world, connect with others, and grow.

ALIGNING THE STARS

Write down your work view and your life view, then check—do they align, or pull in different directions?

DEFINING YOUR QUEST

What truly motivates you—money, impact, creativity? A mix of several? Let's find out.

ADVENTURE STYLE

Track the moments when you're engaged, in flow, and energized… and the ones that drain you. A reality check in real time.

TRAVEL MILES RECORD

Revisit your career so far. Which experiences lit you up? Which ones left you cold?

TRAVEL CLIMATE REPORT

Boredom isn't the only measure. You'll explore the cultural ingredients—like autonomy, teamwork, pace—that make you thrive.

EXPLORER'S SUPERPOWERS

Your "superpowers," broadly defined. What can you do naturally well? What skills do others always seem to seek from you?

TREASURE MAP

Pull it all together into a one-page "you" map—a snapshot of who you are today. This becomes your anchor for the next stage of your journey.

We've arranged the exercises in a sequence that makes sense—but you don't have to follow it religiously. Skip ahead if something grabs you, circle back later to the tougher ones.

Each exercise comes with a worksheet you can download from our website—print them as big as you like, scribble, doodle, make a mess.

P. S. Thinking of skipping one because you already "know" the answer, or it feels too easy—or too hard? Your choice. Just remember: the easy path isn't always the one that takes you somewhere new.

4.2 BASE CAMP CHECK-IN

Before setting out on any new chapter, it helps to pause and take stock. This is your moment to look around, see where you are, and reflect on what's working well — and what's ready for change. Think of it as checking your map and your energy before continuing the journey.

By the end of this exercise, you'll have a clearer view of your current landscape and a better sense of what you want to carry forward into the next stage of your life.

But first, we need to let go of a stubborn myth: *work/life balance.*

The story goes like this: work and life are on opposite sides of a scale, and together they must add up to 100%. More work = less life. More life = less work. Sounds tidy, but it's a trap.

Here's why:

- It limits you to one boring choice—work more or work less.
- It makes you feel guilty no matter what, because "perfect balance" is impossible.
- It treats work and life like enemies, as if one is stealing from the other.

The truth? Work isn't outside of life—it's part of it. Just one piece of the whole.

Instead of a scale, imagine your life as a mix of **four big components**:

Health • Work • Play • Love

No percentages to chase. No "ideal" formula. Just your formula—what's right for you, right now.

THE EXERCISE

You're about to evaluate how you're doing in each of these four areas. Not how much time you spend on them—but how satisfied you feel with them.

HEALTH

This is your foundation. Without it, the rest wobbles. But health isn't just "not being sick." It's physical, emotional, and mental well-being.

For some people, it's yoga, meal planning, running, and annual checkups. For others, it's taking the stairs instead of the elevator, walking the dog every day, and making space for stillness. It can be building healthy habits—or dropping unhealthy ones.

Ask yourself: When you wake up, do you feel ready for the day—or already drained? Do you give your body and mind what they need to thrive, or just enough to get by?

WORK

Work is anything that feels like effort toward a goal—whether it's paid or not. Your job, your side projects, volunteer roles, caregiving—it's all "work."

Sometimes work is a paycheck. Sometimes it's about contribution, achievement, duty, or growth. And sometimes it's a mix. The trick is noticing whether the work you're doing fuels you or depletes you.

Ask yourself: Do I feel proud of what I do? Do I want more challenge, less stress, a shift in pace? Am I doing it because I have to, or because I want to?

PLAY

Play is your joy factor. It's anything you do just because it delights you—no agenda, no "return on investment."

It might be painting, gardening, road trips, reading novels, cooking new recipes, dancing in your kitchen, learning guitar, or trying to beat your grandkids at Mario Kart. Play is the space where time disappears, and you lose yourself in the moment.

Ask yourself: When's the last time I did something purely for fun? Do I give myself permission to play, or do I treat it as a luxury I'll "earn" later?

LOVE

Love is connection—with people, animals, communities, even places. Romantic love counts, of course, but so do friendships, family ties, mentoring relationships, and the bond you feel with your dog, your cat, or your favorite coffee shop barista.

Love is the web of attachments that makes you feel seen, valued, and part of something. It's the difference between "just getting through the day" and feeling like you belong in it.

Ask yourself: Where do I feel most connected and supported? Which relationships feed me—and which quietly drain me?

QUANTIFY

Now, let's quantify these four elements.

How would you evaluate yourself in terms of Health, Work, Play, and Love?

- Rule number one: **they don't add up to 100%.** Having more of one doesn't mean you have less of another.
- Rule number two: **more isn't necessarily better.** You can be happier working less, for example.
- Rule number three: **it's not about hours.** It's not the time you spend on each aspect. It's how you feel about each one.
- Rule number four: it's not an objective measure. **It's how you feel.** You can do "less" than someone else but feel closer to 100%.

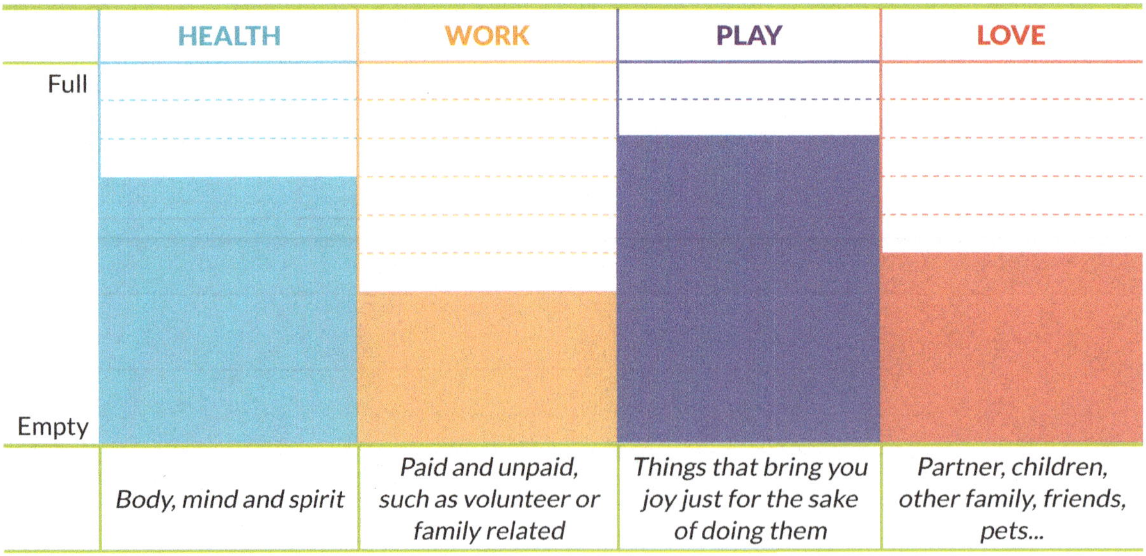

Health can be more important to some people than others. They exercise, watch what they eat, how much they sleep, they meditate. But it's still not enough. Others don't think about it much. But they feel healthy enough.

Just answer these simple questions with a number from 0 to 100%:

- What is your level of satisfaction with health?
- ... with work?
- ... with play?
- ... with love?

What is your level of satisfaction with this overall picture of you?

MY LIFE

You will start with today, your current situation.

This can be considered a quick yet complete dashboard about your life today.

	HEALTH	WORK	PLAY	LOVE
Full				
Empty				

DOWNLOAD

Download the worksheet as a PDF.

REFLECT

Here are a few questions that help your reflection.

- How do you feel about your dashboard?
- Do the four aspects feel balanced or out of balance (you decide what is "balanced")?
- Do you feel good or uneasy about the aspects that are full or nearly full?
- How do you feel about the aspects that are empty or low?
- Which aspects could use action, improvement, or imagination?
- What obstacles do you feel are in your way to improving these aspects of your life?
- What could you experiment with to get a taste for change, that you could then iterate?
- Does a specific problem stand out?

After completing this exercise, you may already have gained insight into what is not working well for you today. You might also have some ideas on how to solve it. If it is the case, experiment with the solution and observe how it works.

If it is still mostly confusing and doesn't seem too illuminating… it is absolutely ok. You are just at the beginning of your journey. Do not dwell on it for too long; move on with the process. You may want to revisit this exercise later.

John

I was surprised to see how little Play showed up for me. But then it hit me—my work is full of playful moments. I laugh, I brainstorm wildly, I meet interesting people. It turns out my job sneaks in a lot of the joy I'd normally call 'play.'

I realized I'd been taking my Health for granted. I'm lucky to feel good now, but that doesn't mean I can coast forever. Small shifts—like cutting out screens before bed—have already made a big difference. I'm sleeping better, and I wake up feeling genuinely rested.

Luisa

Alex

Damn. I definitely have that guilty feeling that my life and work are out of balance.

Thinking of **Health** as a real category was eye-opening. I'm happy with my eating—I've cut down on meat, stopped snacking before bed—but I haven't been exercising and I feel sluggish. My sleep? Not great. I probably need to get serious about a better night routine. On the plus side, I've been working on expressing my emotions—first with my partner, then with co-workers—and it's reduced my anxiety. Still a work in progress.
Score: 70% ⟶ Target: 80%

Work is where I'm overdoing it. I still get into it, but sometimes I wonder if it even matters. That "extra" effort I used to be proud of is starting to feel like overkill.
Score: 120% (yep, over the limit) ⟶ Target: 80%

Play... Do I even play? Do TV shows count? Instagram scrolling? I've been telling myself my play happens at work—but who am I kidding? I need more actual fun. Maybe improv?
Score: 20% ⟶ Target: 50%

Love is my sweet spot. I adore my partner, have a close bond with my kids, and my cat is pure joy. Not a huge circle of friends, but the ones I have are solid.
Score: 90% ⟶ Target: Keep it going.

FEELING
THINKING
INTROVERT
EXTRAVERT
SENSING
INTUITION
Personality

4.3 EXPLORER'S PROFILE

Every great journey starts with knowing who's doing the traveling. This is your chance to look inward — to understand what drives your choices, fuels your curiosity, and occasionally sends you wandering off the planned route.

These insights act like a map of your inner terrain, helping you navigate work, relationships, and change with more ease. When you understand your natural patterns — how you think, decide, and react — you can travel through life with greater confidence and fewer wrong turns.

We'll use the **16 Personalities Test** for this step — a simple yet surprisingly accurate way to see what kind of explorer you are. It only takes a few minutes and might just make you say, "Ah, that explains a lot."

16 PERSONALITIES TEST

Here, we're going to use one we find especially insightful: the **16 Personalities Test**. It's free, quick, and eerily good at making you say, "Wow… yep, that's me."

We won't get bogged down in the theory, but here's the gist: the model looks at **five big elements**, and for each, it places you on a spectrum—not an all-or-nothing box. You might lean one way in certain situations and another way in others.

The five elements are:

- **Mind**
- **Energy**
- **Nature**
- **Tactics**
- **Identity**

Let's peek inside each one.

MIND

This is about how you interact with your surroundings—and where you get your fuel.

On one end, we have **Introverts**: lovers of solitude, rechargers in quiet places, masters of the Irish goodbye at parties. Too much noise, too many people, and they feel like their internal battery is blinking red.

On the other end, **Extroverts**: social dynamos who come alive in groups. They're energized by conversation, thrive on attention, and can be spotted across the room by the laughter and gesturing.

Most of us live somewhere in between. You might be an extrovert at work but turn into a hermit on weekends—or vice versa.

ENERGY

This is how you see the world and process information.

Observant types are grounded and practical. They trust what they can see, touch, and measure. They love facts, routines, and reality checks.

Intuitive types? Big-picture thinkers. They chase possibilities, spot patterns, and often live a few steps into the future. Novelty excites them more than stability.

NATURE

Nature is how you decide—logic first or feelings first?

Thinking types lean on logic, objectivity, and problem-solving. They value efficiency over harmony and often tuck their emotions away.

Feeling types prioritize values, empathy, and cooperation. They read the emotional temperature in a room and aim to keep it warm.

TACTICS

This is how you approach work and decisions.

Judging types love structure, planning, and to-do lists with satisfying little checkboxes. They want clarity, closure, and a plan they can stick to.

Prospecting types prefer to stay flexible, spotting opportunities as they come. They improvise, pivot quickly, and don't mind a bit of chaos if it keeps things interesting.

IDENTITY

This one runs underneath all the others—it's about self-confidence and stress.

Assertive types are steady, even under pressure. They don't over-worry and are fine with "good enough" when it works.

Turbulent types are more self-critical and perfectionistic. They feel stress more sharply—but it also drives them to improve and reach higher.

NOW, YOUR TURN

Head to **16personalities.com** and take the free assessment. You'll get a breakdown of your results, plus a detailed description of your type.

You will also find other useful resources. You can explore the personality traits and their definitions.

Once you have finished the assessment, you will receive the results by email.

Remember: there are no "good" or "bad" results. These are tendencies, not life sentences.

REFLECT

When you read your results:

- Were you nodding in recognition, or were there surprises?
- Did it explain something you've been beating yourself up for—like not being "more social" or not "planning enough"?
- Did you secretly hope for a certain result, thinking it was "better"? (Spoiler: it's not. Every type has its superpowers and its kryptonite.)

Keep these insights in your back pocket. They'll be a handy lens for the next exercises—and for spotting when you're playing to your strengths or fighting against them.

Alex

Personality tests—yeah, I've been around that block. About 15 years ago, I was at this team-building retreat in the middle of nowhere, complete with "trust exercises" that involved far more dangling from ropes than I ever wanted. Somewhere in there, we all shared our personality test results.

Do I remember mine? Nope. Just the takeaway that we're all wired differently, and no type is "better" than another.

So when I saw this test, I went in a bit reluctantly. I braced for something long and dry... but it was actually quick, fun, and—bonus—free. Note to self: dig deeper into the resources on that site.

My result this time? **Campaigner.**
"A true free spirit – outgoing, openhearted, and open-minded."

That's literally the first sentence, and yes, I'm sure they put the flattering stuff up front to hook you. It worked. I read on, nodding along to their description of my spontaneous way of reacting to life.

What really jumped out was the "creative" bit. They kept highlighting it, and I realized—I've had that side locked in a box for years. Probably decades. Responsibilities, "doing the right thing," taking care of my family, ticking all the duty boxes... they've been my default mode. Somewhere along the line, I forgot what it felt like to be free to play, to try, to create without overthinking.

So here's what I'm taking forward:

- **Freedom to explore and experiment.**
- **Shake up the routines.** Try new things just because.
- **Stop pleasing everyone else.** Start pleasing me.
- **Admit I'm not organized.** (Yes, I said it out loud. And no, I don't care.) I'll happily delegate that part.

It's funny—just a little online quiz, but it gave me permission I didn't know I needed.

4.4 ALIGNING THE STARS

Even the best explorers pause now and then to check their bearings. This exercise is your moment to make sure your direction still feels right — not just at work, but in life as a whole.

We often talk about "work–life balance" as if it's a question of time, when really it's about alignment. Are your values, priorities, and daily choices pointing toward the same horizon?

Work isn't the opposite of life; it's part of the same journey. Taking the time to to see how your stars align ensures that the path ahead feels meaningful, not just manageable.

THE TWO VIEWS

You're going to write two short statements:

1. **Your Work View** – what you believe about work in the broadest sense.
2. **Your Life View** – what you believe about life itself.

Then you'll set them side by side, like two travel itineraries, and see where they align, where they clash, and where there might be room for a merger.

WORK VIEW

This is your chance to unpack what "work" really means to you—beyond the paycheck or job title. Ask yourself:

- What is work for?
- Why do I work?
- What makes work feel meaningful?
- What makes good work good?
- What truly motivates me?
- How important is money in the equation?
- How do colleagues and society fit into my idea of work?
- Where do learning, growth, autonomy, and mastery come in?
- What is the meaning of work in my life?

Take your time here. Be honest. If you write something that feels a little uncomfortable, that's a sign you've hit something worth exploring.

LIFE VIEW

Now zoom out. Life is more than the stuff you do for a paycheck—it's the whole messy, beautiful, sometimes baffling picture. Ask yourself:

- What is life about?
- What makes it meaningful?
- What makes it worthwhile?
- Where do love and play fit in?
- How do I see my role in my family, community, or humanity?
- Do I believe in a higher power, and if so, how does that shape my life?
- How do I make sense of joy and sorrow, justice and injustice, love and hate, peace and conflict, and life's random curveballs?

If you had to make a top-three list of what matters most for a fulfilling life, what would be on it? Love? Freedom? Security? Growth? Fame? Knowledge? Don't judge your answers—just write them down.

DOWNLOAD

You can grab the **Aligning Your Stars worksheet** as a PDF to make this process easier.

REFLECT

Once you've written your Work View and Life View, step back and look at them together. Ask yourself:

- Where do they complement each other?
- Where do they conflict?
- Does one drive the other? How?
- What would I want to change to make them work together?

This isn't a neat, one-and-done exercise. You'll probably find yourself jumping back and forth, tweaking both as new thoughts bubble up. That's a good thing—it means you're digging deeper into what you truly believe.

Why this matters: When your Work View and Life View point in the same direction, you stop feeling like you're living two separate lives. You start moving with the wind at your back, not fighting against it. And that makes every step forward feel lighter.

You know what really smacked me in the face during this exercise? My Life View has always included helping others... but my Work View? Nope. For years, my energy was all about helping my family—and honestly, I wouldn't change that. But now that my role at home isn't as front-and-center, I can feel this big, gaping space where "helping" used to be.

It's like there's been a missing puzzle piece sitting right in front of me the whole time, and suddenly it's lit up in neon saying, Pick me!

I've picked up so many skills over my career—stuff I didn't even realize could be useful outside of my job. And now I'm itching to channel all of that into something bigger than me. A cause. A project. Something that actually makes my work and my life point in the same direction.

Alex

4.5 DEFINING YOUR QUEST

Every great adventure starts with a "why." What are you really after — freedom, purpose, creativity, security… or a mix?

Somewhere along the road, many of us were told we couldn't have both meaning and money — that doing good and doing well were two separate paths. It's time to challenge that idea. Life isn't about choosing one perfect route; it's about finding the balance that keeps you moving forward with energy and conviction.

This exercise helps you map what truly drives you today. Because your quest isn't just about what you *do* — it's about what makes the journey feel worth taking.

In this exercise, we'll explore **three driving forces** that show up in most people's work life:

- **Money** – the stuff that pays the bills and buys you the occasional shiny thing you've been eyeing.
- **Impact** – the difference you make, whether it's helping one person, shaping a community, or nudging the world a little closer to "better."
- **Expression** – the creative spark, the "you-ness" that shows up when you're in the flow and your brain lights up.

The mix of these three will look different for everyone. It will shift over time. What mattered most to you at 25 may barely register at 55—and vice versa. And that's okay.

This is your **Quest Map** —your personal recipe for what you "make" and what motivates you to keep making it.

HOW TO DO IT

For each motivation—Money, Impact, Expression—write down what you do, what you want, and how you feel about it. Think of it as a brain dump: no censoring, no trying to sound impressive, no "right" answers.

Pro tip: put today's date on it. If you'd done this 10 or 15 years ago, your answers would almost certainly be different. That's fine. We're interested in *you today*.

MONEY

- What do you do for money?
- What does money mean to you?
- How important is it to have money—or have more money?
- Does money actually make you happy?
- Do you have "enough"?
- Is money a constant worry or background noise?
- When you think about money, what feelings pop up—freedom? security? guilt?

IMPACT

- What do you do that actually makes an impact?
- How do you define "impact"? Is it helping others? Being "a good person"? Sacrificing for a cause?
- Is making a difference—to people, the planet, your community—important to you?
- What "cause" tugs at you?
- Does your sense of impact affect how you feel about yourself?
- When you imagine making a bigger impact, what feelings come up—pride? purpose? energy?

EXPRESSION

- What do you do to express yourself?
- Do you consider yourself creative? (Spoiler: you don't have to be a painter or musician to answer "yes.")
- How do you express yourself—through work, hobbies, conversations, problem-solving?
- How important is it to have space for self-expression?
- When you get to express yourself fully, how does it feel—energized? alive? at peace?

QUANTIFY YOUR BALANCE

Once you've explored each of the three, try to put some numbers on them. On your worksheet, fill in the columns for Money, Impact, and Expression based on how much attention and energy you currently put into each.

There's no "must add up to 100%" rule here. This is your view of your own balance, not a math test.

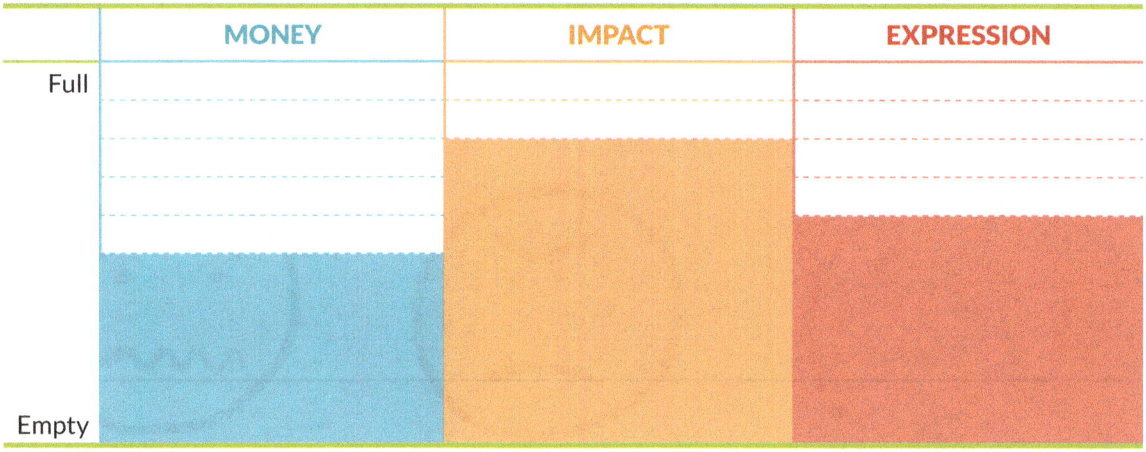

TODAY

Start with your current situation. How does your bar chart look right now?

	MONEY	IMPACT	EXPRESSION
Full			
Empty			

DOWNLOAD

Download the worksheet as a PDF.

REFLECT

- How do you feel about your "Today" chart?
- Would you like to tip the scales toward making more money?
- Would a bigger impact make you feel more fulfilled?
- Do you need more room for creative expression?
- Or do you want less of one of them because it's crowding out the others?

Now imagine your *ideal* balance. How far is it from where you are today?

What's one small step you could take tomorrow to move in that direction? Maybe it's signing up for a weekend art class. Maybe it's volunteering for a cause. Maybe it's saying "no" to one more project at work so you can breathe.

These little shifts—these *first bricks*—are how you start building the life that makes you happy.

	MONEY	IMPACT	EXPRESSION
Full			
Empty			

A dysfunctional belief

"I have to choose: make money OR do something meaningful. I can't have both."

Reframe as

Money **and** meaning are not enemies—they can coexist, and often fuel each other.

I refuse to let the market dictate who I am or what I create.

I choose the blend of money, impact, and self-expression that feels right for me—my own unique Quest.

Alex

Money... yeah, that used to be the driver. It fueled the climb, the hustle, the late nights. It meant I was winning. It meant security for my family—and that mattered more than anything. Now? It doesn't light the same fire. Maybe it's because I'm comfortable enough. Still, there's this old reflex in me that equates money with success. I can feel it loosening its grip, though. Today, it's maybe 80%. In the future? I think 40% will feel plenty.

Impact was always lurking in the background, but not front and center. I remember turning down a job once because it clashed with my values—that felt good. These days, I keep wondering, what if I could make a difference in a bigger way? Not just help companies succeed, but create something that actually matters to people or the planet. Today, I'm at 30%. Tomorrow? Give me 100%!

Expression... honestly, I'm not even sure what that means for me anymore. I've never been "artsy," but I was creative—back in the day. Maybe my expensive watch is a form of expression, but... meh. That's not what I want it to be. I think I need to give myself permission to play more, to try things without worrying if they're "me." Today, maybe 20%. Tomorrow, I'd love to hit 50%.

The truth? I can't magically rebalance overnight. But I can loosen my grip on work (and yes, money) to make room for impact... and see where that might lead.

a+b=c

4.6 ADVENTURE STYLE

Every traveler has a preferred way to explore — some crave the climb, others the quiet path through the woods. The same goes for work and life.

This exercise helps you spot what fuels your energy and what drains it. Think of it as finding your personal rhythm for the road ahead — the kinds of activities that make you feel alive, engaged, and eager for what's next.

Your *Adventure* Style is your guide to choosing what's worth saying "yes" to — and what's better left off the map.

A dysfunctional belief

"Work is not supposed to be enjoyable. That's why it's called work."

Reframe as

Enjoyment is a guide to finding the right work for you.

WAYFINDING: THE ANCIENT ART OF FIGURING IT OUT

Wayfinding is what sailors, explorers, and wanderers have done for centuries—finding their way when they don't have a clear destination.

In our earlier exercise, *Aligning The Stars*, you explored your work and life views. That compass gave you a *direction*. Now it's time to actually start moving and watch for clues along the way.

Think of it like this: you put your destination into a GPS, but instead of a step-by-step map, you're navigating in real life. No perfect road signs, no smooth highways—just you, the clues, and your instincts.

Your two biggest clues?

- **Engagement** — When you're totally absorbed in what you're doing.
- **Energy** — Whether it fuels you or leaves you feeling like you've just run a marathon you didn't train for.

ENGAGEMENT: WHEN TIME DISAPPEARS

Engagement feels like being fully tuned in. You're focused. You're enjoying yourself. You're productive and effective—and it feels good.

Sometimes, engagement kicks into overdrive, and you hit **flow**—that state where time stops. You're not bored (too easy) and you're not overwhelmed (too hard). You're right in the sweet spot, doing something challenging enough to hold your full attention but not so difficult that you're drowning in stress.

Here's the thing: a satisfying career—and a satisfying life—needs a healthy dose of flow. That's when you're at your best.

ENERGY: THE FUEL BEHIND THE FUN

Energy is the other big clue.

Some activities leave you buzzing, even after hours of work. Others suck the life right out of you (hello, pointless meetings). You know that feeling when you've just finished something meaningful and you're ready to take on the world? That's high-energy. And when you walk out of a soul-draining task ready to nap? That's low-energy.

Being able to spot the difference—and design your life around the things that give you more juice—is game-changing.

THEY'RE RELATED… BUT NOT THE SAME

Here's where it gets interesting:

You can be *engaged* but still *drained*. Maybe you loved doing it, but it took everything out of you. Or you can be energized but not that engaged—like when a simple task frees up mental space and makes you feel light.

That's why we look at both separately.

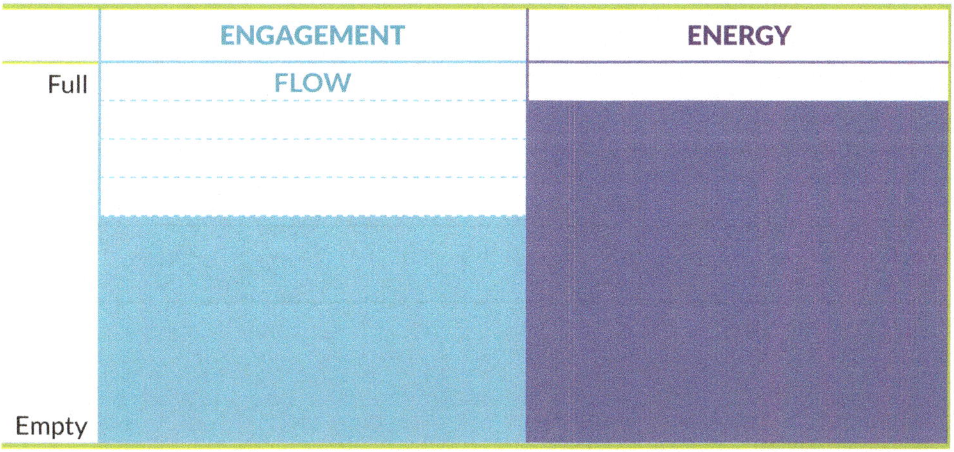

QUICK EXERCISE

Fill in the blanks:

The last time I felt **engaged**, I was doing...

The last time I felt **energized**, I was doing...

YOUR NEW HABIT: ADVENTURE STYLE JOURNALING

This isn't a "sit down once and think about it" exercise—it's a week-long experiment in *self-observation*.

Here's how to make it work:

1. Decide your tracking method.

You can use:

- Our downloadable workbook (print as many pages as you need)
- A plain notebook or journal
- A notes app on your phone
- A spreadsheet (great if you love data and want to spot patterns later)

The tool doesn't matter—what matters is that you can use it quickly and consistently.

DESCRIPTION	ENGAGEMENT	ENERGY

2. Set reminders.

- Keep your tracking method within arm's reach.
- Add a phone reminder for 2–3 times a day so you don't forget.
- You can log after each activity, or do a quick recap at lunch and before bed.

3. For every activity you do, note:

- **What** you were doing (be specific: not just "work" but "wrote report for client" or "had coffee with friend")
- **Engagement level** (Were you bored? Content? Fully in flow?)
- **Energy level** (Drained? Neutral? Energized? Ready to sprint around the block?)
- Optional: Any quick thought or feeling that pops up ("I love when I get to brainstorm" or "Too many interruptions made this painful").

4. Track for at least 7 days.

One week gives you a mix of activities—work, social, chores, hobbies. If you want richer insights, go for 2–3 weeks.

5. Don't judge—just record.

Your job is to notice, not to fix things right away. The magic happens later when you step back and see the bigger picture.

DOWNLOAD

Download the worksheet as a PDF.

REFLECT

At the end of the week (or two), review your entries:

- Which activities score high on both engagement and energy? (These are gold.)
- Which ones are low on both? (These might be worth reducing or redesigning.)
- Do you notice any patterns in the time of day, location, or people involved?

Extra insight: Talk your results through with someone you trust. Sometimes explaining what you wrote helps you connect the dots you didn't even see before.

By the end, you'll have a clear map showing what fills your tank and what drains it—and that's the kind of information that can completely change the way you design your days.

Alex

Damn, I'm not organized. That was long and repetitive. Thank god for my to-do app! I set two reminders—one after lunch, one before bed—just to make sure I didn't forget to jot things down while they were still fresh.

Here are a few highlights from my week:

Day 1

- Meeting preparation – collect data, create slides: Engagement 50/100, Energy 30/100
- Reading articles: Engagement 80/100, Energy 30/100
- Meeting with clients: Engagement 90/100, Energy 90/100

Day 3

- Networking dinner: Engagement 80/100, Energy 100/100
- Week planning: Engagement 20/100, Energy 30/100

Day 5

- Brainstorming meeting: Engagement 90/100, Energy 1000/100! (Yes, I know that's not a real number, but that's how it felt.)
- Reporting and analysis: Engagement 30/100, Energy 20/100

Day 7

- Budgeting: Engagement 10/100, Energy 10/100
- Morning walk in nature: Engagement 90/100, Energy 90/100 (It's funny—by the end of the week I finally started noticing things outside of work!)

By the end, I was actually surprised at how enlightening it was. Totally worth the effort.

Here's what stood out for me:

- I **love** spending time with people—collaborating, talking, exchanging ideas, challenging each other. That's when I feel alive and things actually move forward.
- I **really dislike** working alone in front of my laptop, drowning in data and details. Too much thinking, not enough progress.
- I get bored fast when I'm just "executing" the same task over and over again.

If I learned one thing, it's that I thrive in connection and action—and I need to design my work (and life) so there's more of that and less solitary grind.

culture
vocation
employment
development
hiring
practice
JOB
business
resume
Specialty
profession
money
CAREER
Technology
relationship
FUN

4.7 TRAVEL MILES RECORD

Every traveler has a story in their miles — the routes taken, the detours missed, and the places that left a mark. This exercise is your chance to retrace your professional journey, not to polish a résumé, but to notice the patterns that have shaped your path.

Look for the roles, projects, and experiences that felt meaningful, the ones that taught you something important, and those you'd happily leave behind. Understanding where you've been will help you decide where you might want to go next.

The process is simple: list every job or role you've had—yes, all of them, even that summer gig in college if it taught you something. For each one, jot down:

- **Your main responsibilities** – What did you actually do day to day?
- **The number of years** (or months) you held that position
- **The industry** you were in
- **What you liked** – The good stuff. The moments you felt in your element.
- **What you didn't like** – The parts that made you sigh, procrastinate, or secretly daydream of another career.

Keep it short and snappy. No need for essays—keywords or bullet points work perfectly. This is for you, so you can be totally honest (and yes, "endless pointless meetings" is a valid entry under "disliked").

Remember: this isn't a CV exercise. You're not trying to impress recruiters. You're creating a personal highlight reel to help you understand your own story.

Here's the structure you can follow in the workbook or on a separate sheet:

JOB ROLE	MAIN RESPONSIBILITIES	# OF YEAR	INDUSTRY	I LIKED	I DISLIKED

DOWNLOAD

Download the worksheet as a PDF.

REFLECT

Once you've mapped out your career, step back and take a look.

Do you notice any themes?

- Maybe you've been chasing variety… or stability.
- Maybe you thrive when you're managing people, or maybe you shine when you're deep in creative work.
- Maybe your least favorite tasks keep showing up again and again (and it's time to break up with them for good).

Look for patterns, progressions, twists, and happy accidents. This inventory will be a powerful reference point as you design your next chapter.

4.8 TRAVEL CLIMATE REPORT

Before setting out on any journey, it helps to know the weather — not just outside, but around you. The same goes for work: culture is the climate you operate in every day.

We're not talking about "casual Fridays" or free snacks, but the real atmosphere — the shared values, unspoken rules, and everyday behaviors that set the tone.

Culture is the personality of a workplace. It shapes how people connect, how decisions get made, and how it feels to show up each morning. Understanding that climate helps you recognize the environments where you truly thrive.

It affects:

- How decisions are made (or not made).
- How open people are to sharing ideas.
- How much resistance you'll face when proposing change.
- Whether meetings are productive... or just performative.

You might not always be able to name it, but you can *feel* it. Ever said, *"This place is so political,"* or *"People here actually help each other out"*? That's you talking about **organizational culture**.

WHY THIS MATTERS

Because y**ou thrive in some cultures and wilt in others**. And if you're designing the next chapter of your life, you want to plant yourself where you can flourish.

THE CORE ELEMENTS OF CULTURE

Every workplace falls somewhere on these spectrums:

1. **Formal ↔ Informal** – Dress codes, titles, and strict protocols… or jeans, first names, and casual chats?
2. **Competitive ↔ Cooperative** – Is it all about being *the best*, or about *working together*?
3. **Structured ↔ Unstructured** – Do you follow clear processes, or make things up as you go?
4. **Innovative ↔ Traditional** – Is change embraced, or do people say, *"We've always done it this way"*?
5. **Multinational ↔ SMEs** – Corporate giant with global reach, or small, agile business?
6. **International ↔ Local** – Cross-border collaboration, or deeply rooted in one community?

WORK CULTURE – ORGANIZATIONAL

FORMAL	INFORMAL
• Rules and regulations are clearly written • Autonomy and responsibilities are clearly defined	• Rules and regulations are not written and clear • Autonomy and responsibilities are not clearly defined

COMPETITIVE	COOPERATIVE
• Least amount of interdependence among functions and roles • Meet periodically to share information • Strong focus on individual objectives and achievements	• High interdependence among functions and roles • Continuous sharing of information, team work to plan work, solve problems, make decisions and review progress • Other people share accoutability to meet objectives

STRUCTURED	UNSTRUCTURED
• Usually pyramid shaped, hierarchical and can be depicted in organization charts	• Non-hierarchical or have no clear structure

WORK CULTURE – STRUCTURE

INNOVATION	TRADITION
• Disruptive development • Openness to experimentation	• Incremental product development • Importance of the past business history

MULTINATIONAL	SMES (EUROPEAN DEFINITION)
• Headquarter in one country and its branches are spread across other countries • Both produces and sells goods or services in various countries	• Less than 250 employees

INTERNATIONAL CULTURE	LOCAL CULTURE
• Multicultural • Diversity	• Most of the employees have the same cultural references and experiences

YOUR TURN

For each pair, mark where you naturally sit — not where you wish you were, but where you feel at home.

This is about **preferences**, not "good" or "bad."

FORMAL											INFORMAL
COMPETITIVE											COOPERATIVE
STRUCTURED											UNSTRUCTURED
INNOVATION											TRADITION
MULTINATIONAL											SMES
INTERNATIONAL											LOCAL

DOWNLOAD

Download the worksheet as a PDF.

REFLECT

Once you've mapped your preferences:

- Do they match the cultures of jobs you've loved?
- Do they explain why certain roles drained you?
- Can you already see what kind of environment will help you thrive in your *next* chapter?

Knowing your culture fit isn't just self-awareness. It's a **filter** for future opportunities — a way to say "yes" only to the places where you can bring your best self.

I used to think culture was just... background noise. You know, something you 'adapt' to, like the weather.

But when I listed my past jobs and matched them against those culture spectrums, the penny dropped.

In my favorite role, we were **informal**, **cooperative**, and **innovative**. We brainstormed in cafés, challenged each other without ego, and could test a new idea by Friday. I thrived.

In my worst job? **Formal**, **competitive**, **traditional**. Every email had to go through three managers. People guarded their information like state secrets. Even lunch breaks felt political. I thought I'd lost my edge — turns out, I was just in the wrong environment.

Now, when I picture my next chapter, I'm not just imagining the work. I'm imagining the room I'll be working in, the kind of conversations I'll have, the energy I'll feel when I walk in on a Monday morning.

Culture fit isn't a 'nice to have' for me anymore — it's a deal breaker.

Alex

1

4.9 EXPLORER'S SUPERPOWERS

You have superpowers — yes, you.

And we're not talking about flying or invisibility (though that would come in handy on some days). These are the real kind: the mix of abilities, instincts, and talents that make you effective, creative, and unmistakably you.

The challenge is that most of us underestimate what we can do. We focus on the obvious skills — the ones that fit neatly on a résumé — and forget the quieter strengths that truly move us forward. When your view of your abilities is too narrow, you limit the routes you can take.

This exercise helps you see the full map of your strengths so you can travel with more confidence — and spot new directions you might not have noticed before.

Let's start unpacking your superpowers.

STEP 1 – TECHNICAL COMPETENCIES

We'll start with the easy ones — your **technical skills**.

These are the "hard" skills that are usually listed in your job description. They're the abilities you use to perform specific tasks: accounting, coding, project management, writing, graphic design, running audits, repairing equipment, operating machinery, and so on.

To find yours, pull out your **Travel Miles Record** from the last chapter. Go through each position you've held, and jot down the core skills you used.

Don't list every little thing — focus on 5–10 solid skills that really showcase your career so far.

STEP 2 – CORE COMPETENCIES

Here's where it gets more interesting — and trickier.

Core competencies are **transferable skills** — the ones that show up in *every* job, no matter the industry. Sometimes people call them "soft skills," but they're much more than that. They're your way of thinking, interacting, and approaching problems.

And here's the magic: core competencies can open doors to totally different projects, industries, or even careers, because they aren't tied to one role.

We're going to use the **OECD Common Core Competency Framework** to help you identify yours.

It includes **15 competencies** split into three groups:

1. **Delivery-related** – Getting things done
2. **Interpersonal** – Building relationships
3. **Strategic** – Planning for the future

S
S
S

THE EXERCISE

1. **Read** the list of competencies and their descriptions (in the next section). Don't skim — take time to really understand what each means.
2. **Download and print** the cards from our workbook (or just copy them onto slips of paper).
3. **Sort them** into three piles:
    - "That's me!"
    - "Could be me"
    - "Not me"
4. Keep revisiting the definitions until you feel confident about your choices.
5. From your "That's me!" pile, **pick your strongest competencies** and **rank them**.
6. For each top competency, **write down real-life examples** of when you used it. What was the situation? What did you do? What was the result?

Tip: If you get stuck, do this with a trusted friend or colleague who knows you well. They'll probably spot strengths you take for granted.

DOWNLOAD

Download the 3 worksheets.

DEFINITIONS

The next pages will present the definitions.

DELIVERY-RELATED – ACHIEVING RESULTS

Analytical Thinking is the ability to identify patterns across situations that are not obviously related, and to identify key or underlying issues in complex situations.

Achievement Focus is generating results by assuming responsibility for one's performance and the correctness of one's interventions and recognizing opportunities and acting efficiently at the appropriate moment and within the given deadlines.

Drafting Skills are based on the ability to respectfully communicate ideas and information (often technical) in writing to ensure that information and messages are understood and have the desired impact.

Flexible Thinking involves the ability to effectively adapt to a variety of situations, individuals, or groups. It is based on the ability to understand and appreciate different and opposing perspectives on an issue, to adapt an approach as the requirements of a situation change, and to change or easily accept changes in one's own organizational or job requirements.

Managing Resources is about understanding human, financial, and operational resource issues to make decisions aimed at building and planning efficient project workflows, and at improving overall organizational performance.

Teamwork and Team Leadership implies working cooperatively with others, being a part of a team, and assuming the role of leader of a team. Note that in many cases, people work not only with their own teams, but also with teams and groups across and outside the organization. Therefore, they need to work together effectively with interdependent goals and common values and norms to foster a collaborative environment and drive teams in the same direction.

INTERPERSONAL – BUILDING RELATIONSHIPS

Client Focus is based on the ability to understand internal/external clients' (e.g. committees, working groups, country representatives, etc.,) needs and concerns in the short to long-term and to provide sound recommendations and/or solutions.

Diplomatic Sensitivity implies understanding other people. It includes the ability to hear accurately and understand unspoken, partly expressed thoughts, feelings and concerns of others. Included in this competency is an emphasis on cross-cultural sensitivity. Proficiency in Diplomatic Sensitivity requires the ability to keep one's emotions under control and restrain negative actions when faced with opposition or hostility from others or when working under stress.

Influencing implies an intention to convince others in an honest, respectful and sensitive manner in order to get them to go along with one's objectives. It can also be the desire to have a specific impact or effect on others.

Negotiating involves the ability to work towards win-win outcomes. At lower levels, this competency assumes an understanding of one's counterparts and how to respond to them during negotiations. At the higher levels, the competency reflects a focus to achieve value-added results.

Organizational Knowledge is the ability to understand the power relationships within the Organization and with other organizations. It includes the ability to understand the formal rules and structures, including the ability to identify who the real decision-makers are as well as the individuals who can influence them.

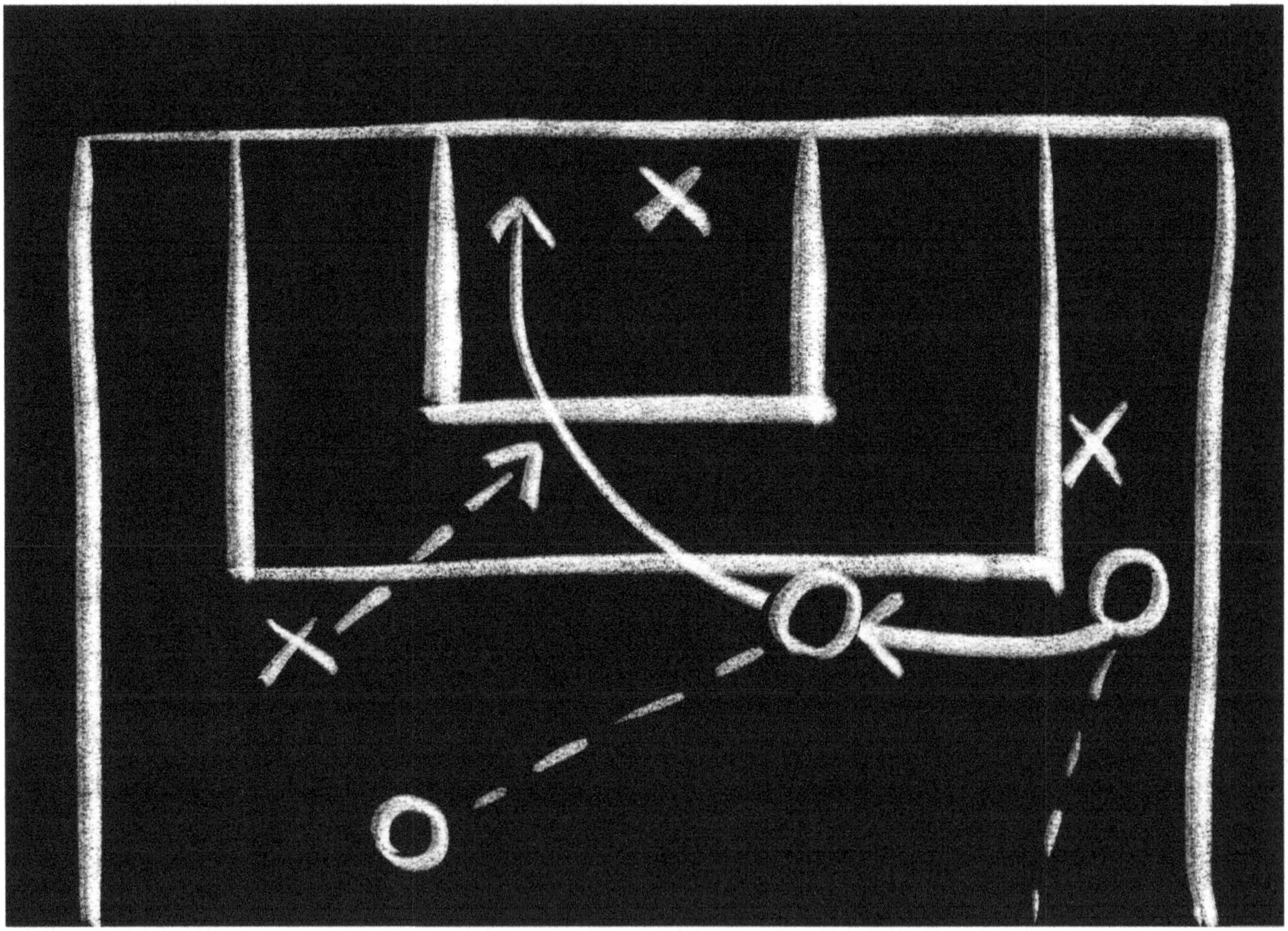

STRATEGIC – PLANNING FOR THE FUTURE

Developing Talent means fostering an environment that will encourage professional and personal growth and the transfer of knowledge to future talent.

Organizational Alignment is the ability and willingness to align one's own behavior with the needs, priorities, and goals of the organization, and to act in ways that promote the organization's goals or meet organizational needs. Organizational Alignment means focusing on the organization's mission before one's own preferences or professional priorities.

Strategic Networking involves working to build and maintain friendly, trustworthy and open internal and external relationships and networks with people who are, or might become, important actors in achieving strategic-related goals.

Strategic Thinking is the ability to develop a broad, big-picture view of the organization and its mission. Competitive advantage and threats, industry trends, emerging technology, market opportunities, stakeholder focus – Strategic Thinking is where these all come together. Strategic Thinking keeps individuals and groups focused and helps decide where to invest critical resources. It includes the ability to link long-range visions and concepts to daily work.

EXPLORER'S SUPERPOWERS

	COMPETENCY	RANK	EXAMPLE
DELIVERY-RELATED	Analytical Thinking		
	Achievement Focus		
	Drafting Skills		
	Flexible Thinking		
	Managing Resources		
	Teamwork & Team Leadership		
INTERPERSONAL	Client Focus		
	Diplomatic Sensitivity		
	Influencing		
	Negotiating		
	Organizational Knowledge		
STRATEGIC	Developing Talent		
	Organizational Alignment		
	Strategic Networking		
	Strategic Thinking		

REFLECT

When you've ranked your competencies, step back and ask yourself:

- Which ones come most naturally to me?
- Which ones have I overlooked or undervalued?
- Did I discover a "hidden" superpower I've been ignoring?
- How could these strengths shape my next project or career move?

Remember, you are much more than your degree or job title.

When you know your full set of competencies, you start to see opportunities everywhere.

That card game exercise? Surprisingly fun. It was like holding up a mirror to my skills — except instead of just seeing the obvious stuff, I started noticing the little things I do almost without thinking.

Two big ones jumped out at me: **connecting people** and **asking great questions.**

I mean, I've always done these. I'm good at them. I enjoy them. They light me up. But here's the thing — no one has ever officially hired me for them. Employers got those skills for free... lucky them.

Now I'm wondering... maybe they are competencies. Maybe even my best ones. And if that's the case, I'd love to bring more of them into whatever I do next. Because they make me happy, they help others — and that feels like a win-win.

Alex

N
W
O
S

4.10 TREASURE MAP

This final step is all about **pulling everything together** — turning all those scattered insights from the past exercises into one clear, inspiring picture of *you.*

Think of it as making **a map of your own territory** — your skills, values, motivators, and dreams. We call it the **Treasure Map**.

Here's how it works:

You'll go back through each exercise and pull out the most important gems — the "aha!" moments, the patterns, the things you want to remember. Then, you'll place them into the corresponding spaces on your Treasure Map.

As you do this, you'll get one more chance to pause, reflect, and let those insights really sink in. You might even spot connections you missed the first time.

When you're done, you'll have a big-picture view of who you are today — your **updated self-portrait**.

Hang it where you can see it. Share it with someone you trust. Let it remind you of the journey you've taken and the strengths you've uncovered.

Because this isn't just a map. It's *your* map. And it's the foundation for the next chapter you're about to create.

DOWNLOAD

Download the PDF.

TREASURE MAP

NAME	
DATE OF BIRTH	
RELATIONSHIP STATUS	
NATIONALITY	
COUNTRIES WHERE I LIVED	
SPOKEN LANGUAGES	

BIO	HOBBIES & INTERESTS

PERSONALITY

EXTROVERTED		INTROVERTED
OBSERVANT		INTUITIVE
THINKING		FEELING
JUDGING		PROSPECTING
ASSERTIVE		TURBOLENT

ALIGNING THE STARS

After completing the exercise, summarize here your most important insights.

GOALS IN LIFE

At this point, what are the main goals you would like to achieve in your life?

PAIN POINTS

MAKER MIX

My Dashboard "Balance"

	MONEY	IMPACT	EXPRESSION
Full			
Empty			

ADVENTURE STYLE

After completing the exercise, summarize here your most important insights.

ENGAGED	FLOW	ENERGY-POSITIVE	ENERGY-NEGATIVE

PROFESSIONAL PATH

CURRENT JOB ROLE ______________ **FROM** ___ **TO** ___

MAIN JOB EXPERIENCES

JOB TITLE	FROM...TO...

INDUSTRIES

TRAVEL CLIMATE REPORT

FORMAL											INFORMAL
COMPETITIVE											COOPERATIVE
STRUCTURED											UNSTRUCTURED
INNOVATION											TRADITION
MULTINATIONAL											SMES
INTERNATIONAL											LOCAL

EXPLORER'S SUPERPOWERS

DELIVERY RELATED - ACHIEVING RESULTS	INTERPERSONAL - BUILDING RELATIONSHIPS	STRATEGIC- PLANNING FOR THE FUTURE	TECHNICAL COMPETENCIES

Wow. Pulling all these exercises together into my Treasure Map was... a lot. Honestly, it wasn't all fun. Some parts felt like therapy, others like homework. There were moments I just wanted to skip ahead—to the "aha" part without slogging through the reflection. But now that I've done it, I get why it matters.

Seeing everything on one page—my patterns, my blind spots, the things that truly light me up—was powerful. It's strange how easy it is to forget who you are when life keeps you on autopilot. Writing it all down forced me to face myself, the good and the not-so-good.

Some exercises hit harder than others. The **Adventure Style** showed me where I come alive. **Aligning The Stars** asked questions I'd been dodging. And **Defining Your Quest**... well, that one exposed a few uncomfortable truths about what I've been chasing.

Was it hard? Absolutely. Worth it? Even more so. For the first time in a long while, I feel like I can see myself clearly—not who I used to be, but who I am right now, and who I want to become next.

Ready to get into the next chapter of the book!

Alex

IMPORTANT

05

What is important to you?

Sometimes the way you see a problem is the real problem. Here you'll learn to step back, remove your blinders, and reframe challenges from new angles—turning roadblocks into design opportunities.

In this part, you'll learn how to **step back, tilt your head, and see your life from fresh angles**. Sometimes, all it takes is a shift in perspective to turn a roadblock into a doorway.

We'll give you tools to:

- **Reframe problems** so they stop feeling stuck and start revealing new solutions.
- Spot the difference between **what you can change *and* what you *can't***—and focus your energy where it matters.
- **Define problems more clearly** (because a fuzzy problem rarely gets a sharp solution).
- Study the "**bright spots**" in your life—the things that are already working—and learn how to grow them.
- Hold up a **mirror to yourself**, and also see through someone else's eyes.

By the end, you'll be ready to rewrite the story you're telling yourself, take off the blinders, and open up to exciting, previously invisible possibilities for your future.

5.1 REMOVING YOUR BLINDERS

You want things to change. You feel it in your gut. But where do you even start?

You're frustrated—though it's not always clear *with what*. You long for something "better"—though "better" is still a bit blurry in your mind.

Here's the catch: before you can move forward, you need to actually see the problem. And that's trickier than it sounds.

Think about listening to a friend unload their problems. They'll leave out key details, oversimplify, avoid taking responsibility, or get stuck in one point of view. You—on the outside—can see things they can't. You might offer a different angle, expand their perspective, and help them spot possibilities they were blind to. All while being supportive.

Now imagine doing that for yourself. That's much harder.

Inside your own head, your stories are biased, selective, and sometimes flat-out misleading. You lock onto a single narrative and cling to it—even if it's holding you back.

This chapter is about breaking free from those mental blinders. You'll learn how to step outside your own head, zoom out, and see your situation with fresh eyes. Think of it as being your *own best friend*—the kind who's both brutally honest and unconditionally supportive.

THE EXERCISES

Here's how we'll do it. This set of exercises will help you spot what's really going on, and—more importantly—open up new ways to respond:

- **Gravity Problems** – Some problems are like gravity: frustrating, but completely outside your control. Others are actionable—you can actually do something about them. The trick is knowing the difference, so you stop wasting energy fighting gravity and start putting your effort where it counts.
- **Problem Statement** – Problems feel obvious in your head, but when you try to explain them, things get fuzzy. This exercise gives you a clear structure for naming your problem. It forces you to get specific, and makes it easier to ask for help.
- **Reframing** – Maybe the most powerful tool in the kit. We all tell ourselves stories about our lives. Those stories usually come preloaded with a "solution"—often the wrong one—which boxes us in. Reframing breaks that loop. It helps you see your story differently, uncover fresh angles, and open doors to better problems—and far better solutions.

WORK

5.2 GRAVITY PROBLEMS

You have problems. I have problems. We all do.

(And you can define "problem" however you like—anything from "I lost my keys again" to "I'm deeply unhappy with my life.")

Here's the thing: some problems you can actually do something about. Others... not so much.

The goal of this exercise is to separate the two. To focus your energy on problems that are *actionable*—where you can realistically design a solution—and to let go of the ones that are simply part of life.

WHY "GRAVITY PROBLEMS"?

Picture this: you sprint up three flights of stairs. By the top, you're gasping for air, your heart's racing, and you mutter: *"Ugh, gravity is killing me. If only gravity didn't exist, I'd float right up these stairs."*

Sounds ridiculous, right? Because there's nothing you can do about gravity.

Sure, you could get fitter, pace yourself, or take the elevator—but gravity itself isn't going anywhere. Fighting it would be a complete waste of energy.

That's exactly how some of life's problems work. They're just part of the system, the environment, the rules of the game. We call these *gravity problems.* The only sane response is acceptance. Stop cursing gravity and move on.

On the flip side, there are *design problems.* These are the ones where you have real agency. You can design a workaround, craft a new approach, or shift your behavior to move closer to a solution.

The real skill here? Learning to tell the difference.

A SPECTRUM OF DIFFICULTY

Of course, life isn't so black and white. Problems exist on a spectrum. Some are technically solvable, but in practice… the odds are so slim they may as well be impossible.

Take me (John), for example. Let's say my dream is to be a rock star. The reality: I'm 62, I've never played an instrument, and I can't sing. Technically, it's *possible*. But realistically? That's a gravity problem.

Another example: when I was 53, I was job hunting. Compared to when I was 30, interviews were scarce. Like it or not, ageism exists in the job market. I could waste energy raging against the system—but that wouldn't land me more interviews. That was a gravity problem I had to accept.

Here's the twist: because I didn't find a job, I started working independently. That led me to a portfolio career I love—and eventually to writing this book. Sometimes what looks like a dead end becomes a doorway.

WHERE YOU HAVE POWER

Think about it like this:

- **Zero power (gravity)** – Laws, systems, aging, red lights. You're not changing them.
- **Some influence** – You can't control the whole system, but you can improve your chances. For example, you can't erase hiring bias, but you *can* prepare better for interviews.
- **Full agency** – In some areas, you're the king or queen. You can quit your job. You can change your routine. You can say no.

The art is knowing where you stand, and putting your energy into the places where you can actually move the needle.

A BONUS INSIGHT

Sometimes, you *can* shift a problem from the "gravity" column to the "design" column.

Remember the stair story? Gravity itself is untouchable. But being out of shape? That's a design problem. By training, pacing, or changing your approach, you reclaim influence.

This book will keep giving you tools to do just that—reframe and redesign problems so you stop fighting the impossible and start building the possible.

A dysfunctional belief

"If I can't solve this problem, I've failed."

Reframe as

Not every problem is mine to solve.

Some problems are just gravity—they exist, whether I like it or not. My job is not to defeat gravity, but to notice it, accept it, and then focus my energy where I actually have influence.

I succeed not by solving every problem, but by choosing the right problems to work on—the ones where I can design, create, and make a difference.

EXERCISE

Grab a pen and paper. Write down a few of the problems in your life—the stuff that frustrates, annoys, or blocks you. Don't censor yourself.

Then, for each one, ask: *Is this gravity, or design?*

If it feels fuzzy, place it somewhere along the spectrum between the two.

The clearer you are, the less energy you'll waste fighting gravity—and the more you'll have for building solutions that actually matter.

PROBLEM	GRAVITY	DESIGN

One of the first things I wrote down was: **"I wish my partner enjoyed the same hobbies as me."** At first, I treated it like a problem I needed to solve. But honestly? That's gravity. I can't change their interests.

What I **can** do is find friends to share those hobbies with, or just enjoy them on my own. And funny enough, once I stopped pushing, my partner actually joined me for a hike. Total bonus.

Alex

5.3 PROBLEM STATEMENT

In the last exercise, you listed some problems.

Now let's be honest: how did you describe them? Probably a little messy, right? Sometimes we leave out important details. Sometimes our "problem" is tangled up with our emotions. And often, without realizing it, we slip a "solution" into the statement that we've already tried (and spoiler: it didn't really work).

Take this example:

Problem: *"I don't go to the gym enough."*

Only solution: *"Go to the gym more."*

But if we dig a little deeper, the real problem might be: *"I am out of shape."*

And that opens up many more solutions than just *"force myself to the gym."*

If you want to find solutions that actually stick, you need to clearly express your problem first. That's where the **problem statement** comes in.

A good problem statement is like a flashlight. First, it helps you see clearly yourself. Things that sound obvious in your head suddenly become harder (but more real) when you write them down or say them out loud. That's progress—it means you're being precise.

Second, it makes it easier to share your problem with others. Once you can explain it clearly, you can talk about it without confusion—and maybe even ask for help.

Here's the key: the problem statement is about the problem, not the solution.

Most of us are trained to jump into problem-solving mode instantly. But when we do, we narrow our options to that very first idea, which often isn't the best one. By separating the problem from the solution, you keep your options wide open. And if you ask someone else for help, you're giving them the chance to bring fresh perspectives instead of just confirming what you already thought.

So let's get practical. A simple problem statement has four parts:

1. You have an aspiration, a goal.
2. But you are stuck. There is a problem.
3. That problem makes you feel something—frustration, pain, anger.
4. And here's an example of how it shows up in real life.

This format forces you to articulate what you want, what's blocking you, how it makes you feel, and an example that illustrates the reality. Often, it's the example that reveals the heart of the problem.

EXAMPLES

Relationships

"I want to get married and have a family. But I never seem to get a second date. I'm frustrated and humiliated. A few weeks ago, I went out with Dominique, and we really hit it off. We exchanged texts for a while, and it was great. Then I suggested a weekend away to meet my parents. It's been a week, and no reply. I kept texting… and now I've been ghosted."

That is a lot clearer—and more useful—than just saying:

"I'll never find someone. People hate me."

Health & Energy

"I'm just tired all the time. Life is exhausting."

vs

"I want to feel more energetic during the day. But I keep staying up late scrolling on my phone, which makes me groggy and unfocused in the mornings. I feel frustrated because I know it's in my control, but I keep repeating the same cycle. Last week, I had to bail on a morning workout (again) because I was exhausted."

Work Satisfaction

"My job sucks. I need a new one. End of story."

vs

"I want to feel proud of the work I'm doing. But lately, my projects feel repetitive and uninspiring. I feel bored and stuck, like I'm not learning or growing. Just yesterday, I caught myself zoning out in a meeting, wondering if this is really how I want to spend the next five years."

Social & Play

"I don't have enough friends. My social life is boring."

vs

"I want to have more fun and connection outside of work. But I keep saying no to invitations because I feel 'too busy' or 'too tired.' I feel isolated, and my friendships are fading. When an old friend invited me to a concert last weekend, I turned it down—and immediately regretted it."

SO LET'S PRACTICE.

Go back to your earlier notes—your list of problems, or even your Work View and Life View—and pull out a few frustrations. Where do you feel blocked? Where do you feel stuck? Where do you find yourself saying, *"I wish this were different..."*

Maybe you didn't get the promotion. Maybe you're bored at work. Maybe you don't have enough time with your kids.

Whatever it is, try writing a problem statement for each one using the four steps:

1. Aspiration (what you want)
2. The problem (what's in the way)
3. The feeling (how it affects you)
4. An example (to ground it in reality)

You have an aspiration, a goal.

But you are stuck. There is a problem.

That makes you feel pain, frustration, anger.

For example, this is how it happens.

2↑

5.4 REFRAMING

What exactly is reframing—and why does it matter?

At its core, reframing is about stretching your perspective. It's the practice of looking at a problem from different angles so you don't get trapped in a single, narrow story. The magic of reframing is that it doesn't just help you solve problems—it helps you solve the *right* problems. Think of it like cleaning your glasses: the issue might be the same, but suddenly you can see it clearly.

Take the classic "**elevator problem.**"

People in a building are constantly complaining: *"The elevator is too slow!"*
The obvious solution? Make the elevator faster. That could mean:

- Replacing the motor
- Reprogramming the software
- Or, in the extreme, replacing the entire elevator system

But reframing asks: *what's really going on here?*
The actual problem isn't the elevator—it's boredom. People are frustrated because waiting feels like wasted time. Once you see that, completely new options appear. You could, for example:

- Hire performers to entertain people in the lobby (a bit wild, but it would work!)
- Or the much cheaper, more practical solution: install mirrors.

Suddenly, people stop complaining—not because the elevator is faster, but because they feel less bored. Everyone likes to see themselves in the mirror.

That's the power of reframing.

If you jump to solutions too fast, you lock yourself into your first, narrow take—and inflate the cost and complexity. Reframing lets you re-describe the issue, which often reveals **better** problems and **smarter** solutions. When you consider multiple standpoints, you generate a wider range of options—and one of them is usually far more interesting than the rest.

That also improves your decision-making: with only a couple of options, the odds of picking the optimal one are slim.

Example: "Should I get an MBA or not?"

Are those really the only two choices? What do you truly want—and *why?* What other paths could deliver that result?

The idea is to:

- **Postpone** grabbing the first solution that pops up.
- **Look with fresh eyes** and try alternate interpretations of the problem.
- **Select the best problem** to solve.
- **Avoid** spending time and money on the wrong one.

Sounds simple. It isn't. We can all list a few options—but how do you reliably find *more*, so your odds of a great answer go up?

There's method to the madness.

Here are five exercises to help you reframe like a boss.

(They're coming next.)

WORKSHEET

We stole* a handy canvas to guide you through the reframing steps. Print it a few times, write the issue you identified at the top, and let's work it from different angles.

** The canvas comes from Thomas Wedell-Wedellsborg's book "What's your problem?" You can find it here:* **howtoreframe.com**.

FRAME

What's the problem?

Who is involved?

REFRAME

Look outside the frame	Rethink the goal	Examine bright spots	Look in the mirror	Take their perspective

MOVR FORWARD

How do we keep momentum?

5.5 LOOK OUTSIDE THE FRAME

Sometimes, the way we define a problem is itself the problem. We put it in a neat little box and forget that boxes have walls. Reframing starts with asking: *what might I be missing?*

When we "look outside the frame," we deliberately widen our perspective. The issue might not be what we first thought it was. Maybe it's influenced by history, by hidden assumptions, or by something happening just outside our field of vision.

Take the classic example of declining sales. The knee-jerk frame is: *our product isn't good enough, so we need to improve it.* But what if the real issue isn't the product at all? Maybe it's that customers don't even know it exists. Or maybe their buying habits shifted because of a new trend, regulation, or competitor move. Improving the product won't help if the problem lies elsewhere.

Looking outside the frame means asking fresh questions:

- What events led up to this?
- Who or what is influencing the situation that I haven't considered?
- What's unusual here? What doesn't quite fit?
- If I were from a totally different field, how would I see this?

A hospital once struggled with patients missing appointments. The obvious frame: *people are careless or forgetful.* But when they looked beyond, they realized transportation was the hidden issue. Patients couldn't easily get there. By reframing, the hospital introduced shuttle services—and no-show rates dropped dramatically.

The trick is to challenge your first definition of the problem. Expand it. Question it. Turn it around. Sometimes the most useful insight is sitting just outside the edge of the picture.

Quick exercise: Think of one problem you wrote down earlier. Now ask yourself: *What am I not seeing? What's outside the frame? What hidden factor could be shaping this issue?* Write down three new angles.

FINISH

5.6 THE END GOAL

Here's another simple but powerful tactic to help you reframe: instead of obsessing over the problem, focus on the *end goal*—the deeper thing you actually want.

A FIRST EXAMPLE

Let's say you're worried about not getting a promotion.

At first glance, it seems clear: your problem is the promotion. But let's peel back the layers.

- You want the promotion because you want a higher salary.
- You want a higher salary because you want to send your kids to a better university.

See what happened? The real goal isn't the promotion—it's paying for your kids' education. And once you frame it that way, your options multiply. A side job, cutting expenses, scholarships, downsizing, even the half-joke option of marrying a rich person! None of those are possible if the "problem" is defined as just one narrow solution: *get the promotion.*

When you keep the real aspiration in mind, you suddenly open the door to more creative solutions.

ANOTHER EXAMPLE

Mary loved her job but had a terrible boss. She thought her only option was to quit—despite loving everything else about her role. A headhunter helped her reframe: her true goal was not to quit but to keep loving her work. So they found a new job… for her boss. Mary stayed, the boss left, and she kept the job she loved.

YET ANOTHER ONE

An airport worked hard to speed up passengers' walk from the gate to baggage claim. They cut the time in half. Success? Not quite. Passenger complaints *doubled.* Why? Because passengers got there faster, but still had to wait for luggage. Before, the walk ate up some of that wait. The total time was the same, but satisfaction plummeted.

The airport solved the wrong problem. If they had looked at the *end goal*—passengers feeling the wait was reasonable—they might have focused on making the waiting area more engaging, or synchronizing luggage delivery instead of speeding up the walk.

FINAL EXAMPLE

You're fed up with your job. You feel stuck, not learning, not progressing. The problem feels like: *I must quit.* But maybe your real goal is to keep learning. That opens up new ideas: carving out time for side projects, seeking out training, trying new tools, or proposing experiments within your role. Quitting is one option, but not the only one.

QUICK EXERCISE

Pick one issue from your own list. Now ask: *what's the higher objective here?* If you step back, what's the real thing you're after? And does that shift the way you see possible solutions?

OMG, I complain so much about things I can't change—or that don't even matter all that much. It's like a habit. Just venting for the sake of venting.

This chapter hit me. The idea of stepping back, looking at the real goal before jumping into half-baked solutions—that's huge. I made a long list of my so-called "problems," and when I looked closer, most of them melted away. What I really want is pretty simple: to live more in the present, to enjoy my life, to put my energy into what actually matters.

Now it's about experimenting with ways to feel energized and aligned. Not chasing fake problems—just focusing on the real goal.

Alex

5.7 EXAMINE BRIGHT SPOTS

When we're stuck, our minds love to zoom in on the problem. We analyze it, dissect it, complain about it. And yes, that matters—but it's only half the story. The other half? Looking at the *bright spots*. The times, places, or situations where the problem *wasn't* there, or when things actually went well.

Instead of asking only, "What's wrong?" try also asking, "When did it *work*?" Those little exceptions can hold the key to bigger change.

EXAMPLE: STRESS

You're constantly stressed at work. Every day leaves you drained and exhausted. That's the story in your head. But wait—was it *every day*? Think back. Maybe two Tuesdays ago, you actually felt good. You were engaged, energized, maybe even enjoyed yourself. That's a bright spot. What was different that day? Was it your task list? The people you worked with? The environment? Or simply your mindset? Spotting that difference can give you a clue for how to redesign more days like that.

EXAMPLE: MOTIVATION

A company struggles with low motivation. Everywhere, employees are checked out—except one team. That team is consistently upbeat, engaged, thriving. Why? What are they doing differently? Maybe it's how they communicate. Maybe it's the freedom they have. Maybe it's their leader. Whatever it is, that "bright spot" isn't just luck—it's a model that can spread.

EXAMPLE: CULTURE

A call center faced an uphill battle dealing with callers from all over the world—different languages, cultures, and ways of expressing themselves. Training programs weren't solving it. Then the talent officer realized: hotels face the same challenge, and they've cracked the code. Instead of reinventing the wheel, the company shifted hiring practices to target candidates with international hospitality backgrounds. Problem solved by borrowing from another industry's bright spot.

The lesson? Your problem probably isn't unique. Somewhere, someone has found a way through. If you can't spot a bright spot in yourself, your team, or your company, widen the lens. Post about it. Ask your network. People *love* to share solutions when they know it might help someone else. You'll be surprised how much more feedback you get when you ask for help than when you brag.

Got passed over for a promotion again? Others have too. Some eventually got it—how? Maybe they took a course, maybe they built a mentor relationship, maybe they shifted roles first. The path is rarely invisible—it just might be hiding in someone else's bright spot.

QUICK EXERCISE

Think of a recurring problem you face. Now flip the lens: when was it *less bad*—or maybe even good? What was different in those moments? And what can you borrow from that bright spot to light up more of your future?

5.8 LOOK IN THE MIRROR

Here's a tough one—maybe the toughest. **What's your part in the problem?**

When something goes wrong, our reflex is to look outward. Who messed up? What broke? Whose fault is it? But here's the catch: we're often part of the equation. Sometimes in big ways, sometimes in small, subtle, even unconscious ones.

Take my friend Mark (not his real name, but he knows who he is). He used to complain nonstop that his kids were glued to their devices. He'd scold them, set limits, even ban screens. But then it hit him—he was always on his phone, too. If he wasn't modeling the behavior he wanted, how could he expect a different outcome?

That's what looking in the mirror is about. It's asking: *What is my contribution to this problem?*

Maybe you didn't create the whole mess, but you're adding to it. Or at least, you're not making it better. And that part—the part you own—is the piece you can actually change.

One trick is to scale the problem down into something manageable. If it feels like a giant, immovable "gravity problem," zoom in. Is there a smaller slice of it that you *can* influence? Maybe not the entire system, but your corner of it. Maybe not the whole conflict, but your reaction in it. Narrow the scope until you find your handle.

And remember—it's not only about *you* personally. Sometimes it's "the mirror" for your team, your department, your organization. How are we part of this problem? How do we make it worse—or could start making it better?

Of course, seeing yourself clearly isn't easy. Our blind spots are… well, blind. That's why it helps to ask for help. Invite someone you trust to be brutally honest. Ask questions like: How do you see me in this? How do I come across? What role might I be playing that I don't notice? What biases could be shaping me? How am I influencing outcomes without even realizing it?

It takes courage to face those answers—but that's where growth starts. Because once you spot your part in the problem, you finally have something real you can do about it.

I'll be honest—this one stung. My first thought was: **Me? Part of the problem? No way.** But then I thought about how often I complain about meetings being unproductive... while I show up late, half-prepared, and usually multitasking. Ouch. That's on me.

Looking in the mirror made me realize I can't just blame "the system" or "other people." My behavior feeds the problem, too. And if I change my part—if I show up ready, stay present, contribute—it might not fix everything, but it will definitely help. That's the piece I can own.

Alex

6
9

5.9 TAKE THEIR PERSPECTIVE

Here's a shift that can change everything: what happens if you stop looking only through your own lens, and try seeing the problem through someone else's eyes?

I've lost count of how many times I've heard technical folks grumble about their "clueless" boss. *They don't know the tech. They don't understand the details. They make dumb decisions.* But here's the thing—the boss's job is different. They don't need the same depth of technical mastery. Their strengths might be elsewhere: building relationships, managing politics, securing resources, guiding the bigger picture. From their vantage point, those skills matter just as much—if not more—for the project's success.

Taking their perspective doesn't mean agreeing with every choice they make. It means acknowledging that their reality, priorities, and pressures are different from yours. And when you factor those in, their decisions often look less irrational and more… reasonable.

This isn't just about bosses, of course. Any problem has multiple actors, each with their own stake. Teammates, clients, family, even people you disagree with—they all see the world through their own filter. If you can step out of your tunnel vision and slip into their shoes, the view changes dramatically.

The tricky part is emotions. When we're excited about an idea or convinced we're right, it's easy to project our certainty onto everyone else. *Of course this is the best path! How could anyone not see it?* But they don't share your exact history, values, or motivations. And that doesn't make them selfish or stupid. It just makes them human—with their own valid perspective.

ANOTHER EXAMPLE

You propose an exciting new idea to a client, but they immediately push back, asking for a simpler, less innovative approach. You think: *They're just being difficult. Don't they see the potential?*

From their perspective, though, they're accountable to their board, with limited budget and high personal risk if things flop. To them, your "brilliant" idea looks like gambling with their career. Once you see that, you can reframe your pitch in a way that addresses their fears, showing how the new idea actually *reduces* risk.

So here's the challenge: be generous. Assume the people across from you aren't villains, but individuals with different needs, pressures, and viewpoints. Give them the benefit of the doubt. Most of the time, what feels like resistance or incompetence is really just a different way of seeing the same situation. And if you can understand *that*, you'll not only defuse conflict—you'll make better decisions together.

5.10 REFRAMING CHECKLIST

When you're facing a tough problem, it's easy to get stuck circling the same thoughts. A reframing checklist is like a toolbox—you don't need every tool every time, but picking the right one can make the job much easier.

Here's a list of reframing strategies you can run through when you're stuck. You don't have to tick every box—just choose the ones that spark new ideas or shift your thinking.

PROBLEM STATEMENT

Start simple:

- You have an aspiration
- But there's a problem
- That creates "pain"
- For example, it looks like this...

Writing it down this way forces clarity.

LOOK OUTSIDE THE FRAME

What might you be missing?

- Look beyond your own expertise
- Look back to prior events that shaped the issue
- Look for hidden influences that aren't obvious
- Spot non-obvious angles or players in the situation

Sometimes the real insight comes from outside your usual field of vision.

RETHINK THE GOAL

Is the goal itself part of the problem?

- Clarify your higher-level goals
- Challenge the logic: does this even make sense?
- Ask if there are other ways to reach the same outcome
- Don't just question the big goal—check the sub-goals too
- Remember: sometimes the "obvious" goal isn't the right one

EXAMINE BRIGHT SPOTS

Are there positive exceptions you can learn from?

- Have you solved this problem at least once before?
- Are there outliers in your team or network doing it well?
- Who else (inside or outside your circle) deals with this issue?
- What happens if you share the problem widely—does someone already have an answer?

LOOK IN THE MIRROR

How are you contributing to the issue?

- Explore your own role honestly
- Scale the problem down to something you can act on
- Ask others for an outside view—how do they see your influence?

TAKE THEIR PERSPECTIVE

What's the world like from the other side?

- What problem are *they* really trying to solve?
- Try to escape your own emotions and step back
- Assume there's a reasonable explanation behind their behavior

DOWNLOAD

Download the documents as a PDF to keep them handy.

5.11 REFLECT

Reframing isn't just a clever trick—it's a mindset you can carry into every corner of your life.

Next time you run into a problem, resist the urge to charge straight at it. Instead, pause. Step back. Ask yourself: *Am I even looking at the right problem? Could there be another angle I haven't considered?*

You'll be surprised at how often this shift opens new doors—revealing hidden options, turning roadblocks into detours, and helping you "solve a better problem" rather than wrestling with the wrong one. It's a habit that makes decision-making sharper, less frustrating, and far more creative.

If you'd like to dive deeper into reframing, one of the best resources out there is Thomas Wedell-Wedellsborg's book *What's Your Problem?* It's a fantastic guide to mastering this skill in both work and life. You can learn more here: **howtoreframe.com**.

BINARY OPTIONS

Here's another trap to watch for: problems are often presented as if there are only two possible solutions. This "either/or" framing can be intentional (to push you toward a choice) or unconscious—but either way, it boxes you in.

Think of a friend saying:

"Come out for drinks with me and meet people. Otherwise, you'll just sit at home alone."
If those were really the only two options, it would sound pretty convincing. But of course, life is rarely that simple. You could meet people in countless other ways—or even enjoy a perfectly fulfilling evening on your own.

Parents know this trick well. To get a child to wear a hat in winter, they'll ask: *"Do you want the blue hat or the red hat?"* The child feels like they're choosing, but the "no hat" option has been cleverly removed from the frame.

That's the power—and the danger—of binary options. The way a question is phrased can dramatically narrow your thinking. The challenge is to step back, notice when you're being squeezed into a false either/or, and ask: *What other options am I not seeing?*

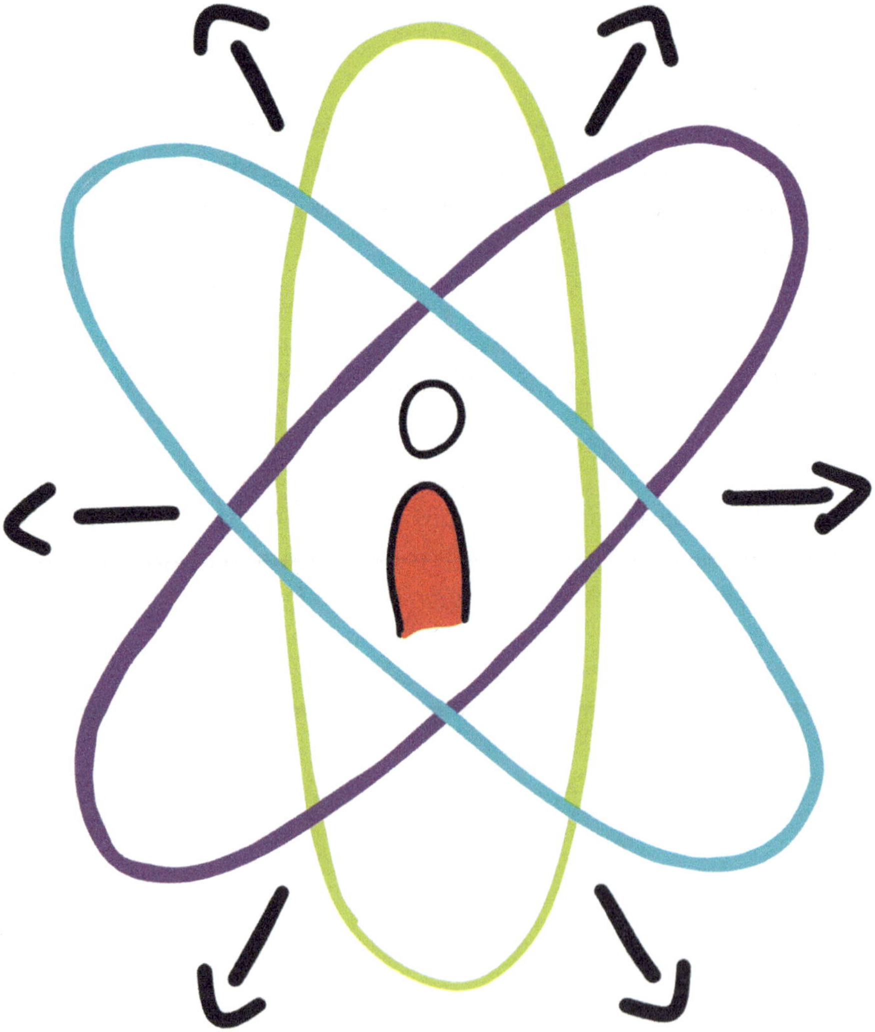

06

You have more possibilities than you think

Your life isn't limited to a single path. In this chapter, you'll brainstorm bold options, explore "what ifs," and design three radically different Adventures—so you can see just how many futures are open to you.

So far, you've been doing the groundwork: mapping out who you are, what matters to you, and how you see the world. Think of it as packing your backpack. Now it's time to step out the door and start exploring.

Here's the fun part: you have *way* more possibilities than you realize. Most of us walk around with blinders on—telling ourselves there are only two or three paths forward. Stay in this job or quit. Go big or play safe. Success or failure. But life isn't a straight hallway with two doors—it's a wide-open landscape with hidden trails, secret passages, and detours you haven't even noticed yet.

This section is about discovery. You'll learn to open your field of vision, spot opportunities in unexpected places, and let your imagination run a little wild. Some of the options you uncover will feel obvious in hindsight, others might seem bold—or even ridiculous. That's okay. The goal isn't to pick the "right" path right now—it's to see just how many paths there really are.

Because the more possibilities you see, the freer you are to design a future that feels exciting, meaningful, and *yours*.

6.1 WHAT YOU ARE GOING TO DO

You've gathered insights, reframed problems, and started to see yourself with new clarity. Now it's time to do something exciting: **turn possibility into play**.

Now comes the fun part—time to roll up your sleeves and start experimenting with tools that will spark new ideas and open fresh paths for you. Think of this as filling up your backpack with gear you'll use on the bigger adventures ahead.

The first tool is a general one for your toolbox. It's designed to help you *connect your dots differently*—to notice patterns you hadn't seen before, to mix and match ideas in surprising ways, and to combine elements of your life into brand-new possibilities.

And then, before this chapter is over, we'll play. You'll actually start sketching and designing possible futures for yourself.

WHERE TO PLAY

This is where we warm up your imagination. You'll take your skills, your competencies, your past experiences, and place them into different contexts. What would they look like in another industry? Another role? A totally different kind of project?

Companies often use this "Where to Play" framework to explore new business opportunities. Here, you'll use it to explore *personal opportunities*—new spaces where *you* could thrive.

DESIGN YOUR ADVENTURE

This is the big one—the most important exercise not only in this chapter but maybe in the whole book. "Design Your Adventure" is where you map out several radically different versions of your future.

You'll set aside the idea of one "right" path and instead sketch out multiple paths—different lives you could lead in the coming decades. Some may feel safe, others bold, and maybe one or two a little outrageous. That's exactly the point.

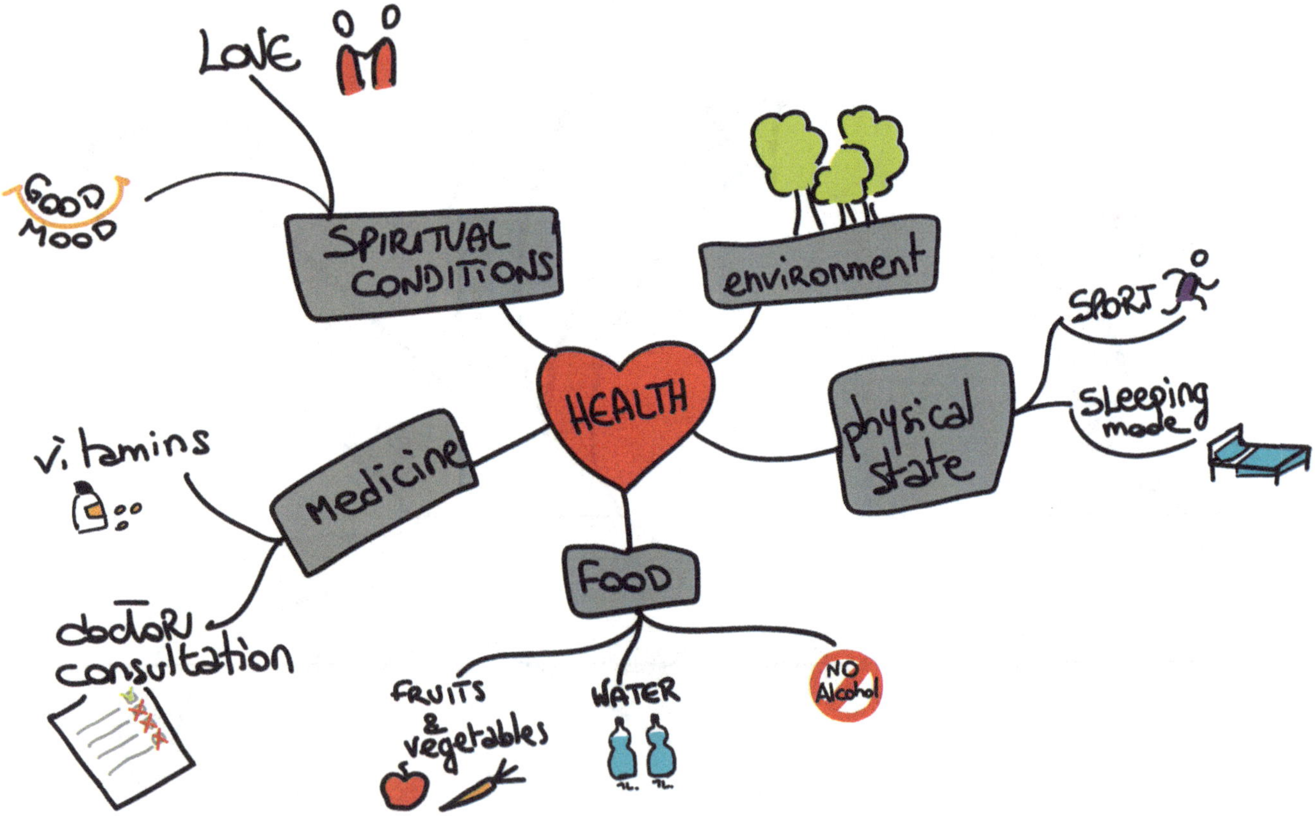
LOVE
GOOD MOOD
SPIRITUAL CONDITIONS
environment
SPORT
physical state
SLeeping mode
HEALTH
vitamins
medicine
FOOD
doctoR consultation
FRUITS & vegetables
WATER
NO Alcohol

MIND MAPPING

Here's a tool that will become your best friend in this process.

Our thoughts often arrive in bursts—half-formed, exciting, overlapping. If you try to capture them in neat, linear notes, you risk losing the magic. But if you let them fly away without writing them down, they vanish.

Mind mapping solves this. It lets you capture ideas visually, in clusters and branches, without interrupting your flow. You'll see connections you didn't know were there—and keep your creativity alive instead of stifling it.

We recommend using it throughout this chapter and beyond.

By the end of this chapter, you'll not just be reflecting on possibilities—you'll be sketching them out and seeing what your future could actually look like.

To learn more about Mind Mapping, go to **our companion website**.

A dysfunctional belief

"I must figure out the one perfect life, map it all out in advance, and then stick to the plan."

Reframe as

There isn't just one perfect life waiting for me—there are many possible great lives I could live. My job isn't to find the one, but to explore, choose, and keep building the version that excites me most right now.

6.2 WHERE TO PLAY

"Where to play" is a method companies use to spot fresh opportunities*. They look at their assets, their technologies, their strengths, their clients, and their networks—and then imagine new ways to put them to use.

We're going to do the same thing, but with you.

You've collected a whole set of assets too: your personality traits, skills, competencies, strengths, quirks, and experiences. You've been using them in a particular way, in a particular career. But what if you applied them somewhere else? A different industry, a different role, a totally different context? How else could you leverage your unique mix of qualities?

IMAGINE

Picture this: a close friend of yours, someone you know really well. You spend time together, share hobbies, maybe play sports or travel together. You know what they're good at, how they think, their strengths—and their quirks.

But imagine they've *never once* told you what they do for work. Based only on what you know about their personality and talents, you could probably guess a handful of jobs that would suit them, right?

Now flip it. Do the same thing for yourself.

The method and book "Where to play" are by Marc Gruber and Sharon Tal - Learn more at* **wheretoplay.co.

HOW TO PLAY

Go back to your **Treasure Map**. Even better, invite a few friends who know you well (but ideally not work colleagues). Show them your Map and let them brainstorm: *If you didn't already know my job, what kinds of careers would you guess for me?* You'll be surprised how they see you—sometimes in ways you've been blind to.

If you'd rather not involve others, here's a trick: use **self-distancing**. Pretend you're brainstorming for someone else—"What could John do?" Or imagine you're advising a friend who just happens to be *exactly* like you. Somehow, when we reframe ourselves as another person, it gets easier to think outside the box.

The goal isn't to pick a new career right now. It's simply to generate **alternative paths** that fit your skills, personality, and way of thinking. What industries might benefit from someone like you? What problems could you be great at solving? What job titles could you hold in a different world?

DOWNLOAD

Download the worksheet as a PDF.

REFLECT

We often trap ourselves in the narrow story we've been telling for years: *This is who I am. This is what I do.*

But when you step outside that story—even just for a moment—new doors appear.

What ideas came up for you (or from your friends)? Which ones surprised you? Did it spark a sense of excitement or curiosity? Did it make you wonder: *Why not me? Why not that?*

I could sense a pattern emerging!

The ideas my friends threw out weren't about technical wizardry or crunching numbers—they were about people. All those interpersonal skills I'd quietly downplayed—listening, connecting, motivating others—suddenly looked like superpowers in a different light.

They saw me thriving in roles where impact is front and center: coordinating volunteer work, leading community projects, working with a non-profit, or even starting my own initiative from scratch. At first, I laughed it off—me, running an association? But the more I thought about it, the more it clicked.

I've always enjoyed bringing people together, creating momentum, and helping others shine. Maybe I just hadn't considered those as "real" skills because no employer ever listed them in a job description. But now I can see how powerful they could be if I put them at the heart of what I do next.

Interesting? Absolutely. A little scary? Sure. But also energizing. For the first time in a while, I caught myself thinking: I could actually do this.

Alex

N
S

6.3 DESIGN YOUR ADVENTURE

Now that you've stretched your imagination with the last exercise, it's time for the big one—the most powerful exercise in this whole process.

An *adventure* is a long journey, full of wandering, discoveries, and unexpected twists of fortune.

We hope yours will be long and meaningful.

We hope your wandering feels like freedom rather than being lost.

And we hope your fortune comes in the form of joy, fulfillment, and maybe even a few happy surprises.

Of course, no adventure is a straight line. You'll need course corrections, detours, and rest stops along the way. But that's exactly what makes it rich and worthwhile.

And then there's the other half of the name: *planning*. Wandering doesn't mean drifting aimlessly. It means setting off with some direction, a sense of where you'd like to head, even if you don't know every turn in advance.

So the real questions are: What's your first step? Which direction do you want to point yourself in?

In this exercise, you'll imagine not just one possible future, but several—some realistic, some bold, maybe even a little crazy. This is your chance to step back, dream freely, and let your imagination sketch out what could be next.

HOW?

You're going to map out your next five years. Year by year, imagine what happens. What are the key events, milestones, decisions, accomplishments? What choices shape each step of the way?

And here's the twist: you won't just do it once. You'll do it *three times.* At least.

Why? Because imagining only your "perfect" future is a trap—it limits you. The real power comes from opening your mind, wandering into different possibilities. Exploring multiple options always leads to better decisions.

One of your plans will probably come easily. You might already carry it in your head as *the* plan. That's fine. Write it down.

But then you'll create two more. At least. And these are where the magic happens. Think of them as alternate voyages—different paths through your life, with fresh crossroads and bold choices. Push yourself beyond what feels safe or obvious. Let yourself play, experiment, even dream a little wildly.

FIVE BOXES FOR FIVE YEARS

Think of this as your storyboard. Each box represents a year in your future.

For each Adventure you design, sketch out what life could look like year by year. What's happening? What choices are you making? What milestones show up along the way?

Don't worry about being precise or realistic—this is not a contract, it's a sketch. The point is to see your possible futures take shape on paper, one year at a time.

A dysfunctional belief

"I'm stuck"

Reframe as

I'm not stuck—I always have the ability to create new options. The more ideas I generate, the more possibilities open up.

You're not making three slightly tweaked versions of the same safe plan.

You're creating **three truly different paths**—each one a bold alternative future.

The **FIRST Adventure** is the "continuity plan." It stays close to your current reality. Think of it as the path you're already on, with some upgrades, tweaks, and improvements. Same story—just a few better chapters.

The **SECOND Adventure** is your "what if the rug gets pulled out" plan. Imagine your job disappears, your profession is obsolete, and you're out on the street. (Yes, after cursing, sulking, and complaining a bit.) Then... you dust yourself off and move on. What would you do? Where would you turn? This plan is all about resilience and reinvention.

The **THIRD Adventure** (our personal favorite) is your "no-limits" plan. Dream wildly. Imagine money is no object. Imagine there's no shame, no fear of failure, no worry about looking ridiculous. No reputation to protect. What would you dare to do if you were absolutely free?

FOR EXAMPLE:

Maybe one plan builds on your engineering skills, another leans into your gift for connecting with people.

One could start with the question, *"What if my profession disappeared tomorrow?"* forcing you to reinvent yourself completely.

Perhaps one version has you finally pivoting to your dream job—or chasing that childhood fantasy you tucked away years ago.

Another could be a life of travel and adventure, or one where you dedicate yourself to a cause that truly matters. Or maybe it's the story where you start your own business.

There could be a version where money is no object. Or one where reputation doesn't matter—you're free to look bold, weird, or even a little crazy.

And yes, there could even be a plan where you stay home, tending a garden and enjoying simple days with your partner.

So, which of these sparks something for you? Which one makes you pause, smile, or feel a little pull? That's the trail worth following.

DO IT

The first one is always the hardest—after that, your imagination starts to flow.

Grab a sheet of paper (or your favorite notebook) and sketch out a future. Don't overthink it—just start.

BRING IT TO LIFE

Start with a title—no more than six words. Short, punchy, to the point. What's the essence of this Adventure?

Now, sketch the journey. Year one, year two, year three, and so on. What needs to happen first to set you on track? Do you go back to school? Change cities? Start therapy? Launch that side project?

6-WORD TITLE

JOURNEY

	0 100
RESOURCES	
CONFIDENCE	
LIKEABILITY	
COHERENCE	

THREE QUESTIONS

1	
2	
3	

Each box is yours to play with. Use words, doodles, arrows, symbols—whatever helps you see it. Pictures often capture the feeling better than text. Remember, this isn't just about work. Think health, play, love, adventures.

Don't worry if it's not perfectly clear. You'll have open questions—capture them. What do you still wonder about? What would you need to explore or test before committing?

GRADING TIME

Then step back and put on a practical lens. Rate your plan on a scale of 1 to 100:

- **Resources:** Do you have the money, skills, time, and network to pull this off?
- **Likeability:** Do you actually like this path? Does it excite you?
- **Confidence:** Do you believe you could really do it?
- **Coherence:** Does this plan fit with what you know about yourself? Does it align with your stars?

You can add extra filters too:

- **Geography:** Where would you live?
- **Learning:** Would you grow as a person?
- **Impact:** Would this make a difference—for you or for others?

Finally, zoom in: what would a typical day look like in this future? Zoom out: what would your life look like?

THREE QUESTIONS

Every Adventure you design is more than just a possible future — it's a way to **learn something about yourself.**

Each plan holds a few questions that you're curious to explore, even if you don't yet have the answers. Think of them as guiding stars — the curiosities that pull you forward.

What are you hoping to discover through this plan? Maybe it's about testing a dream, or finding out whether a different rhythm of life could fit you. Maybe it's about impact — asking, "Would I really feel fulfilled helping others in this way?" Or maybe it's more personal: "Could I actually enjoy slowing down?" "Would this lifestyle energize me or drain me?"

These aren't yes-or-no questions. They're invitations to notice, to observe, to prototype small steps and see what happens.

Writing them down keeps your plan alive and intentional. It reminds you that you're not chasing the *perfect answer* — you're exploring, experimenting, and learning what truly matters to you. Each plan will answer different questions, and that's the point. The more you explore, the more clearly you'll see which future feels right.

What are your three questions ?

REMARKS

1. **This is the linchpin**. Don't skip it and don't phone it in.
2. **Sketch fast**. Don't overthink—messy beats perfect at this stage.
3. **Design your whole life**. Not just work. Remember **Health**, **Play**, **Love** (and Work).
4. **Make one gloriously wild plan**. If none feels risky, you're playing too safe.

TIME TO START

- Prep **three big sheets** and draw the canvas on each (or print the template if you can go big).
- Set a **timer: 15 minutes per Adventure**. Pens out, no erasing, keep moving.
- **Have fun**. Put on music, loosen up, let your thoughts flow.

DOWNLOAD

Download the worksheet as a PDF (then copy it much much bigger).

6-WORD TITLE

JOURNEY				

	0 100
RESOURCES	
CONFIDENCE	
LIKEABILITY	
COHERENCE	

THREE QUESTIONS	
1	
2	
3	

REFLECT

Now that you've sketched out three different Adventures, step back and take a curious look at them.

Which one sparks excitement? Which one feels heavy and draining?
Which path seems most realistic, and which one is wildly out there—but maybe thrilling in its own way?

Don't judge too quickly. The goal here isn't to crown a winner but to notice your reactions. Pay attention to where your energy rises, where you feel resistance, and what surprises you. Those signals matter.

Alex

My third Adventure is bold: I want to make the world a better place.

Title: **Building Hope: A Safe Place**

I've seen firsthand the pain of children who suffered abuse or violence at home. It breaks my heart—and it lit a spark in me. My dream is to open a center where these kids can feel safe, supported, and begin to heal.

Year one starts with two things that matter deeply: first, an unforgettable trip with my partner and kids before they head off to university. That family experience comes first. At the same time, I'll dive into research—what centers already exist, what services are most impactful, and what it really means to help children in these situations.

Year two is about building my foundation. I'll go back to school to finish my psychology degree, strengthen the skills I'll need, and start networking with people already in the field. I'll shape a clear vision, outline a plan, and draft a budget.

Year three brings change at home—moving with my partner into a smaller place as the kids leave—and change in the project. I'll focus on partnerships, collaborations, and fundraising.

Year four is launch year. The center opens. I'll build a team, create the right environment, and take the first steps toward impact.

Year five is about growth—developing programs, building awareness, and spreading the word about an issue that matters deeply to me.

Of course, I have questions: How will I handle the emotional weight of working every day with abused children? Will I really make an impact? Am I ready for the responsibility of running an organization like this?

When I score myself, it looks like this:

- **Resources:** 70. A decent start, but there's work ahead—especially around legal issues.
- **Likeability:** 100. I love this.
- **Confidence:** 30. Honestly, I wonder if I can really do it.
- **Coherence:** 80. This fits my Compass. It feels aligned with who I want to be.

It's daunting. But it excites me more than anything else I've imagined.

6.4 WRAP-UP

There isn't just one "best life" waiting for you — there are many possible lives and paths, and you get to choose which one to build next. By now, you've drafted three five-year Adventures, and that's already a powerful step.

From experience, we've seen people mix and match elements from their different plans, some pivoting big things, others adjusting small details. Some people generate ideas quickly, while others take more time to let them unfold. Both ways are perfectly fine.

Chances are, you won't follow any single plan exactly from beginning to end. But that's not the point. What matters is that you now have sparks, directions, and possibilities worth exploring.

And if you feel stuck or uninspired — that's useful information too. It simply means you need to loosen up and let the ideas flow more freely. The fix? Sketch another Adventure! And then another. Each new draft is a chance to dream bigger, stretch further, and design what would truly make you happy. Remember: on paper, everything is possible.

07

Role-play your future life

Don't just imagine your future—try it on for size. You'll prototype your ideas through interviews, networking, storytelling, and visioning, so you can test what excites you and what really fits before you commit.

It's showtime—you're stepping onto the stage of your future. But don't worry, this isn't opening night. It's rehearsal.

You've designed your Adventures—now it's time to take them off the page and into the real world. In this part, you won't just imagine your future—you'll prototype it. Just like designers build quick mock-ups to test ideas, you'll create low-stakes experiments to see what your next life could actually feel like.

You'll pitch your vision out loud, map the key people who could help or challenge you, and even role-play conversations with them. You'll imagine the headlines announcing your success, test your riskiest assumptions, and collect insider knowledge from those already living the life you're curious about.

Think of it as dress rehearsal. You get to try on different versions of your future, see which ones fit, tweak the script, and toss out what doesn't work—before you commit for real.

By the end, you won't just have a plan. You'll have lived small pieces of your future already—and that makes the leap from idea to reality a lot less scary (and a lot more fun).

7.1 HOW ARE WE GOING TO DO THIS?

So, how do you prototype your life? After all, it's not like you can hold your future in your hands the way you test-drive a new phone or car. But you *can* create small experiments that let you peek behind the curtain before making a big leap.

COFFEE SHOP EXAMPLE

Say you're tired of your banking job. You spend your free time in cozy cafés, sipping your favorite [insert drink here] with a [book, laptop, or friend]. Hours melt away, and you think: *"This is it—I'll quit everything and open a coffee shop!"*

But hold on. Is running a café as relaxing as being the customer? Probably not. So how do you try on the role of coffee shop manager without investing your life savings?

Easy: talk to the people already doing it. Ask your favorite café owner what their days really look like. Or, better yet, volunteer to help out for a week—even unpaid. You'll quickly learn if the dream matches reality.

JOB SHIFT EXAMPLE

Not all changes are about radical reinvention. Maybe you'd rather stay in your company or industry, but move up a level, shift roles, or join a different department. Sounds good... but promotions don't always mean "better." More responsibilities might bring less interesting work. The new team might not click. The dream job could feel like a nightmare.

So, prototype it. Have coffee with someone who's already in that role and ask what they actually do all day. What's exciting? What's frustrating? Spend some time with the team you'd be joining—informal lunches, casual chats, anything that lets you see how they interact.

Sure, shadowing or trialing the job for a week isn't always possible, but you'd be surprised. Some companies are open to it, especially if you frame it as professional growth.

The point is simple: don't leap blind. Find small, low-risk ways to step into the life you're considering. The more you know now, the better choices you'll make later.

EXERCISES

Think of this part like a video game: you've picked your favorite quest (your Adventure), and now you're gathering the tools, maps, and side-missions that will help you win. Each exercise is a different side quest that gives you new powers and insights for the adventure ahead.

Now comes the fun part—you'll take your favorite Adventure (the one that makes your heart beat faster, or simply the one that feels most doable) and start exploring it in the real world.

But before you head out, let's walk through a set of exercises that will make your investigation richer, sharper, and a lot more effective. Think of these as tools for your explorer's backpack.

STAKEHOLDERS

Who are the people that matter for your journey? Some will be your biggest cheerleaders, others may just provide key information, and some might become active players in your future. Mapping them out gives you clarity on who to engage and how.

VALUE PROPOSITION & ELEVATOR PITCH

Can you explain your idea in a way that sparks curiosity? Whether you've got two minutes in an elevator or a full hour over coffee, you'll learn how to talk about your project so people lean in instead of tuning out.

COVER STORY

Now for a leap of imagination: picture yourself five years from now, featured on the cover of a magazine. Which one? What's the headline? What's the story they're telling about you? This exercise helps you think bigger, and frees up your creativity in surprising ways.

RISKIEST ASSUMPTIONS

Every big plan hides a few big unknowns. What do you need to learn before taking the next step? This part is about surfacing those assumptions and figuring out how to test them before they trip you up.

CONVERSATION TRACKER

Finally, it's time to get out there and talk to people. You'll learn some tricks for finding the right contacts, having great conversations, and keeping track of what you discover. This is how ideas turn into reality—through real, human conversations.

7.2 STAKEHOLDERS

Big, life-changing projects rarely happen in isolation. They're often complex, multi-step journeys, and along the way you'll be crossing paths with plenty of people.

And that's the point: **you are not alone in this**. People matter.

In business, we'd call them *stakeholders*—anyone who has a stake in the project. Clients, suppliers, partners, influencers, sometimes even accidental bystanders.

Your future life plan has stakeholders too.

Some will look a lot like business stakeholders if your plan involves work or entrepreneurship. But many will be much closer: your partner, your family, your friends, the people who will be directly touched by your choices.

If you can understand these people—their motivations, their needs, even their language and standards—you'll not only design better plans, you'll communicate them more effectively.

SO, WHO REALLY COUNTS AS A STAKEHOLDER?

Here's the simplest definition: **a stakeholder is someone who gives value to you and/or receives value from you**.

Let's walk through Alex's Adventure as an example.

Alex

Year 1 – An incredible vacation with my partner and kids before they head to university. Family as stakeholders: we exchange value in love, attention, and shared experiences.

Year 1 (continued) – Researching options for helping abused children. Stakeholders: professionals in the field, researchers, and organizers of similar initiatives who can share insights. Also, friends who can provide perspective.

Year 2 – Back to school to study psychology.
Professors: delivering knowledge and skills.

Year 2 (continued) – Networking with like-minded people to build a vision, plan, and budget.
Ecosystem members: exchanging information, support, and experience.

Year 3 – Downsizing the house as the kids leave, while building partnerships and fundraising.
Partners and donors: providing services, funds, and resources.

Year 4 – Opening the center and building a team.
Stakeholders: the children and families receiving support, and the team delivering it.

Year 5 – Expanding and raising awareness.
Other organizations and prescriptors: generating visibility and legitimacy.

ALEX'S STAKEHOLDERS

That gives Alex a pretty comprehensive list:

- Family
- Friends
- Organizers of similar offers
- Professionals in the field
- Researchers
- Professors
- Ecosystem members
- Partners
- Donors
- Beneficiaries and their families
- Their team
- Other organizations and prescriptors

MAP YOUR STAKEHOLDERS

Now it's your turn. Go step by step through your Adventure and jot down the people and organizations that will affect your success—or be affected by it.

This list becomes your compass for the early stages of investigation. The first names that show up—people already living the kind of life you're considering—will be especially valuable. They can give you a true picture of what daily reality looks like. And the stakeholders that show up early in your journey are often the first ones you'll need to reach out to.

So grab a pen, revisit your plan, and start your list.

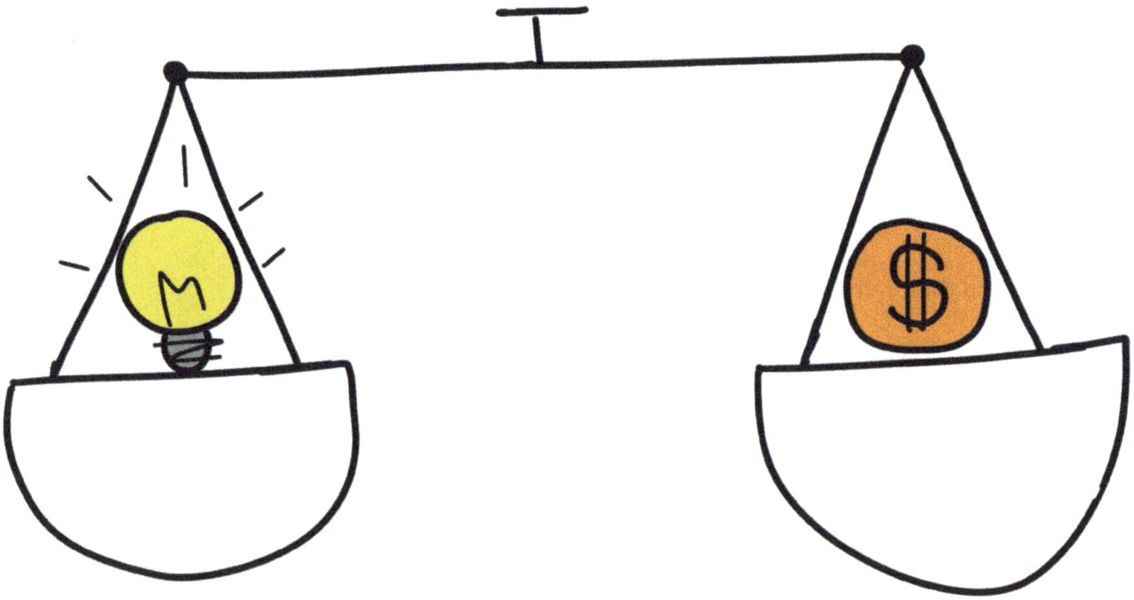

7.3 VALUE PROPOSITION

Value comes in all shapes and sizes. Sure, money matters. But so do things like knowledge, recognition, autonomy, joy, growth, belonging, entertainment, confidence, even status.

At the heart of any plan is a value proposition. In plain terms: **you're offering someone something they value**. Sometimes that "someone" is you. Sometimes it's your family, your clients, your team—or a mix of all of them.

By digging deeper into your *value proposition*, you'll start to see your plan more clearly. You'll stress-test it, refine it, and probably make it stronger.

STEP 1: IDENTIFY THE MAIN BENEFICIARY

Who's the "client"?

Sometimes it's obvious. For Alex, it's the children she wants to support. For you, maybe it's the customers who'll visit your future coffee shop.

Other times, it's less clear. Say you want to shift into a new role at work—your "client" might actually be your manager or the company itself. If they don't see the value, your idea won't fly.

Most plans are born out of a problem. The clearer you define the problem, the easier it is to see who benefits from your solution. And don't forget: there are often *secondary beneficiaries* too. Your family might gain more time with you. Your team might enjoy a better workplace. Your community might get a new resource.

Pick a few key stakeholders and walk through their perspective.

STEP 2: TAKE THEIR STANDPOINT

The trick is to look at the world through their eyes. Three simple but powerful questions will help:

WHAT ARE THEY TRYING TO ACCOMPLISH?

What are their aspirations? Their goals?

Sometimes it's very practical and down-to-earth.

- I go to the hairdresser to get a haircut.
- I hire a gardener to mow my lawn.
- I sign up for a gym to exercise.

But behind almost every practical need hides an emotional driver.

- I go to the hairdresser not just to trim my hair, but to look attractive, feel confident, and walk out with a spring in my step.
- I hire a gardener not just to save time, but to feel proud of my home when friends visit.
- I go to the gym not just to sweat, but to feel healthy, in control, and proud of my discipline.

These emotional layers are often the real goals. People want to:

- feel safe, respected, or admired,
- have fun and escape stress,
- learn something new and grow,
- connect with others and not feel alone,
- or simply get a moment of peace in a chaotic day.

Think about how they will measure their success. Is it in numbers—money earned, tasks completed, goals ticked off? Or is it in feelings—joy, relief, pride, connection, excitement? What kind of experience are they really after?

WHAT IS THEIR PROBLEM?

Why can't they accomplish what they're trying to do on their own?

If they could do it easily, they wouldn't need your help, your service, or your idea.

So ask:

- What's in their way? Time, money, energy, lack of knowledge, lack of tools?
- What frustrates them? A long commute, constant distractions, poor service, bad communication?
- What keeps them up at night? Fear of failure, financial insecurity, the sense that they're missing out?
- What makes them feel embarrassed or ashamed? Not knowing the right jargon, not being fit enough, not keeping up appearances?
- What triggers anger or annoyance? Waiting in line, unreliable technology, people wasting their time?

And dig into the consequences: what's the worst thing that could happen if they never solve this problem? Losing credibility? Losing opportunities? Feeling stuck?

WHAT BRINGS THEM JOY?

Beyond just solving their problem, what lights them up?

Yes, success itself brings joy—but what else? Surprise and delight often come from the little extras they didn't expect.

- The café not only has good coffee, but the barista remembers their name.
- The online course is not just useful but fun, with unexpected bonuses.
- The gym doesn't just offer machines but creates a community where they feel they belong.

Think: what would make their life easier, lighter, or more joyful? What would make them smile and say, *"Wow, that was better than I expected"*?

COFFEE SHOP EXAMPLE

Goal

A professional wants a quiet, productive space to work.

Problem

The commute to the office is long and draining. Home is full of distractions. Pubs are too loud, restaurants won't let you linger, and the Wi-Fi is spotty.

Joy

Wide tables, comfy chairs, reliable internet, plenty of outlets, good coffee, and maybe the chance to meet like-minded people.

YOUR TURN: THE STAKEHOLDERS OF YOUR ADVENTURE

For each of your key stakeholders, run through the same three questions. No need for a full psychoanalysis—just focus on how they relate to your plan.

- What do they want?
- What's in their way?
- What would make their life better?

Rinse and repeat for each person who matters.

WHY DOES THIS MATTER?

When you understand your stakeholders' standpoint, three things happen:

- You talk about your project in a way that grabs their attention.
- You refine your plan so it actually serves their needs better.
- You open the door to stronger support and collaboration.

Sometimes it's as simple as realizing—hey, maybe my coffee shop needs *better Wi-Fi.*

DOWNLOAD

Grab the worksheet as a PDF.

REFLECT

Did this exercise give you a clearer way to talk about your idea? Could you have used it earlier, back when you were shaping your plans?

7.4 TELLING YOUR STORY... SHORT VERSION

At some point, you'll need to *talk* about your plan. Whether it's with a friend, a mentor, a potential partner, or just someone curious at a party—being able to explain it clearly and in a way that sparks interest is essential.

But here's the challenge: you only have a few seconds before people's attention drifts. So how do you hook them? You tell a *short story*—one that paints a picture and makes them feel the need for your idea.

Here's a simple framework you can use:

- **These people...** (Who is it for?)
- **Have an aspiration...** (What do they want?)
- **But have a problem...** (What's in the way?)
- **Which makes them feel...** (What's the pain?)
- **I/We help solve it...** (What's your offer?)
- **Avoiding a bad outcome...** (Optional, but powerful)
- **And making their life better.** (The happy ending!)

You might notice the beginning feels familiar—it's basically the **problem statement** reshaped into a mini-story.

Example: For a gardener:

- Homeowners
- Want a beautiful yard
- But it takes too much work, so their lawn is overgrown
- They feel frustrated
- GreenPlace offers a regular service to keep their garden pristine
- Avoiding the embarrassment of messy yards in front of the neighbors
- And making them proud (and happy!) to spend time at home

See how it takes the listener on a little emotional ride?

- Aspiration = up
- Problem = down
- Solution & positive outcome = up again

That's why it works.

YOUR TURN:

For each of your Adventures, write your short version story. The more you practice it, the easier it gets to share your vision with excitement—and the more likely people are to lean in and say: *"Tell me more."*

COVER STORY VISION CANVAS

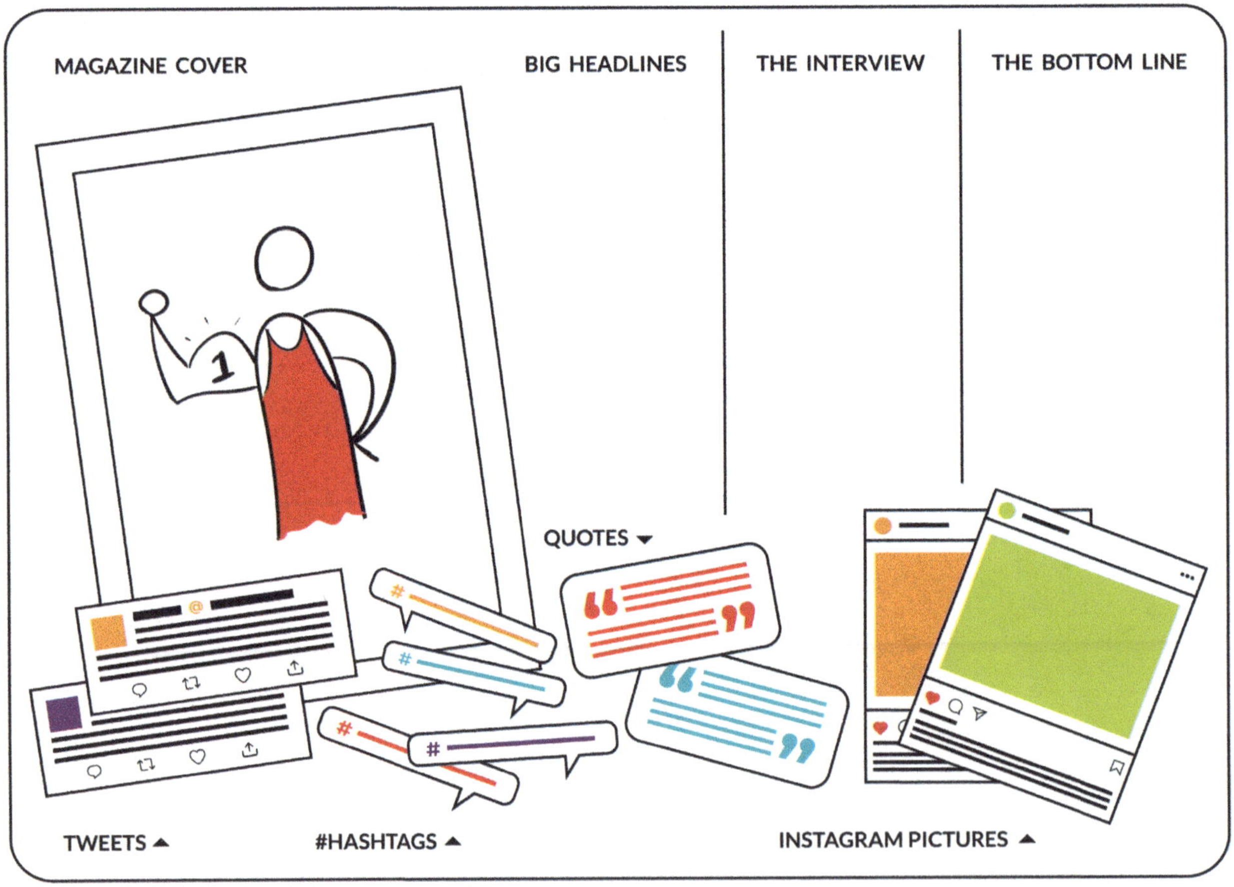

7.5 COVER STORY VISION

Time to jump into the future—and see yourself shine.

This exercise is about projecting yourself into the life you want, and imagining what it looks like once you've *made it*. By stepping forward in time, you'll uncover hidden desires, motivations, and even steps to take today.

Pick your moment. It could be five years from now. It could be when you turn 65 or 75. Choose a milestone that feels inspiring.

Congratulations! You've made the cover of a (prestigious) magazine! We are so proud of you.

But here's the fun part:

- **What magazine is it?** *Is it Forbes? Wired? Runner's World?* A parenting magazine? Your local community newsletter? Maybe it's a niche publication only people in your dream field would know about.
- **What's the story?** Why are they putting you on their cover? What did you accomplish? What impact did you make?

Get creative:

- What photo do they use for the cover?
- What's the big, bold headline?
- What's the interview about?
- What's the financial, social, or personal impact they highlight?
- What quotes, tweets, or Instagram posts would people share about you?

Download the canvas and have fun filling it out. Let your imagination run free—this is your chance to play with bold possibilities.

REFLECT

How did that feel? Did it excite you? Surprise you? Scare you a little?

We spend so much energy on “today” that we rarely allow ourselves to imagine “someday.” This exercise gives you permission to dream—and those dreams can start guiding your choices now.

Wow, that was fun! Seeing myself on the cover felt both surreal and energizing.

What struck me most was how clearly the exercise showed me why my project matters. Thinking like a journalist forced me to step outside myself: What's the headline? What impact would people actually celebrate? What stories would inspire others?

It gave me a new perspective on what's essential—and what's just noise.

Now I feel a stronger pull: this isn't just a dream to imagine, it's a story I want to make real.

Alex

7.6 RISKIEST ASSUMPTIONS

You've got a plan you're excited about. Great! Now it's time to stress-test it a little.

Right now, you probably have parts of your plan that feel rock-solid, others that feel shaky, and still others you haven't even thought through yet. That's normal. The goal here isn't to figure everything out today—it's simply to identify the unknowns that matter most.

Think of it like preparing for a road trip: you don't need to know every street name on your route, but you do need to make sure the car has fuel, the tires aren't flat, and you packed your wallet.

ASSUMPTIONS

Your plan is based on a - potentially long - series of assumptions.

Every plan rests on a pile of assumptions, big and small. For example:

- You'll land that job.
- You'll meet the right people.
- Your family will support you.
- You'll enjoy the day-to-day tasks.
- You'll find the right location.
- Your logo color will be perfect.

IMPORTANT & FUZZY

Two words will guide you here:

Important. If this assumption is wrong, does your whole plan collapse?

Fuzzy. How much do you *really* know about it?

Example: You dream of running a coffee shop. Loving the daily grind (pun intended!) of managing one is **very important**—but since you've only ever sat there sipping cappuccinos, it's also **very fuzzy**.

RANK THEM

Take each assumption and score it:

- Importance: 1 (meh) → 10 (critical)
- Fuzziness: 1 (clear as day) → 10 (no clue whatsoever)

So "enjoying the daily coffee shop routine" might be a 9 in importance and a 7 in fuzziness.

MAP THEM

Now grab a big sheet of paper and draw a grid:

- X-axis = Importance
- Y-axis = Fuzziness

Stick each assumption where it belongs. Don't overthink it—just place it quickly.

WHAT DOES IT LOOK LIKE?

In the beginning, it could look something like this.

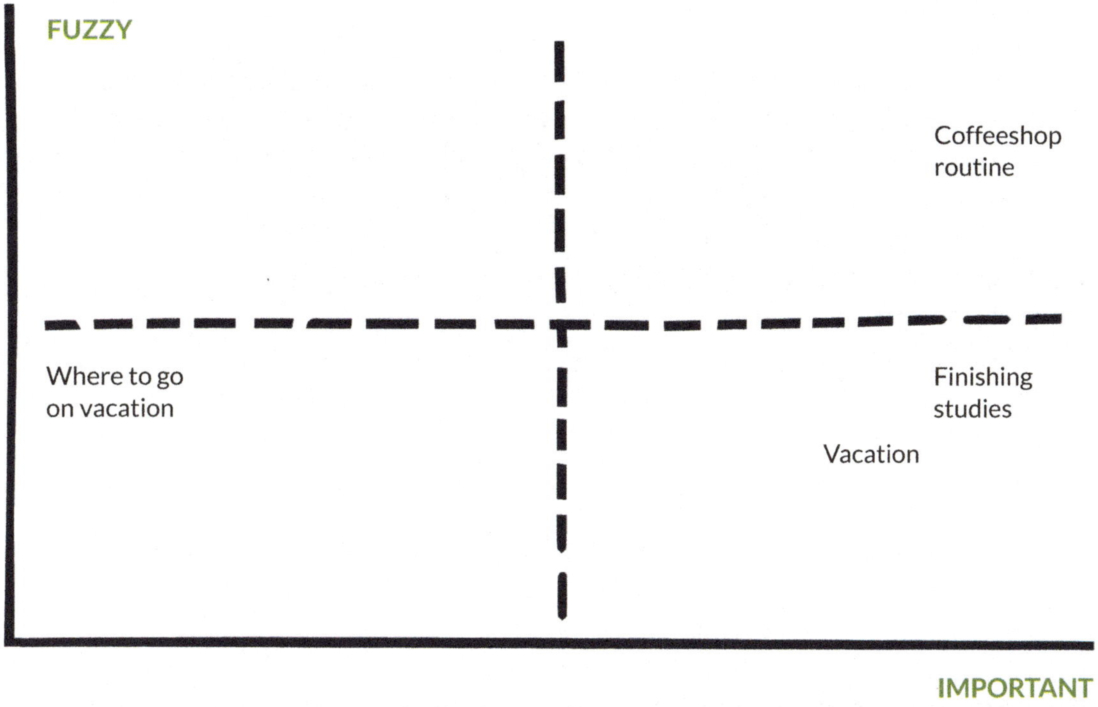

Alex

When I started mapping my riskiest assumptions, things got interesting.

One big one: Can I really handle the emotional weight of working every day with abused children? That's a **10 in importance**—if I can't handle it, the whole project collapses. And honestly, it's still pretty fuzzy.

Another: Will I find enough funding? Without money, there's no center. Again, very important. Fuzziness? High. I've never written a grant or managed fundraising at this scale.

Some assumptions felt less risky. Will my family support me? That's important, but I know them, we've talked about it, and they're behind me—so it sits low on the fuzziness scale.

Putting these sticky notes on the map really helped. I can see clearly now where I need to learn more—especially around emotional resilience and funding—before I go too far.

START LEARNING

Your danger zone is the **top-right corner**: the assumptions that are both really important and super fuzzy. That's where you need to start digging.

- Interview someone in the role.
- Shadow them.
- Test it out yourself if possible.

The goal is to move those sticky notes *downward* (less fuzzy) or even *leftward* (less important).

THEN WHAT?

As you investigate, three things might happen:

- You gain clarity → fuzziness goes down.
- You realize it's less important than you thought.
- Or—you discover it's a deal-breaker. Better to know now than after you've invested years.

When the top-right quadrant is empty, congrats—you've cleared a huge milestone in making your plan real.

HOW

A good way to do it is on a big paper board with post-it notes. As you progress, you can move the notes down and to the left. When the top right quadrant is empty, that's a big step.

A FEW EXAMPLES

- That promotion you're chasing—are you sure it comes with a raise, or just more work?
- That "creative" job—will you actually create, or just manage creatives?
- That move abroad—do you actually enjoy the culture, or just the idea of it?

These are the kinds of **fuzzy-important questions** that make or break your plan.

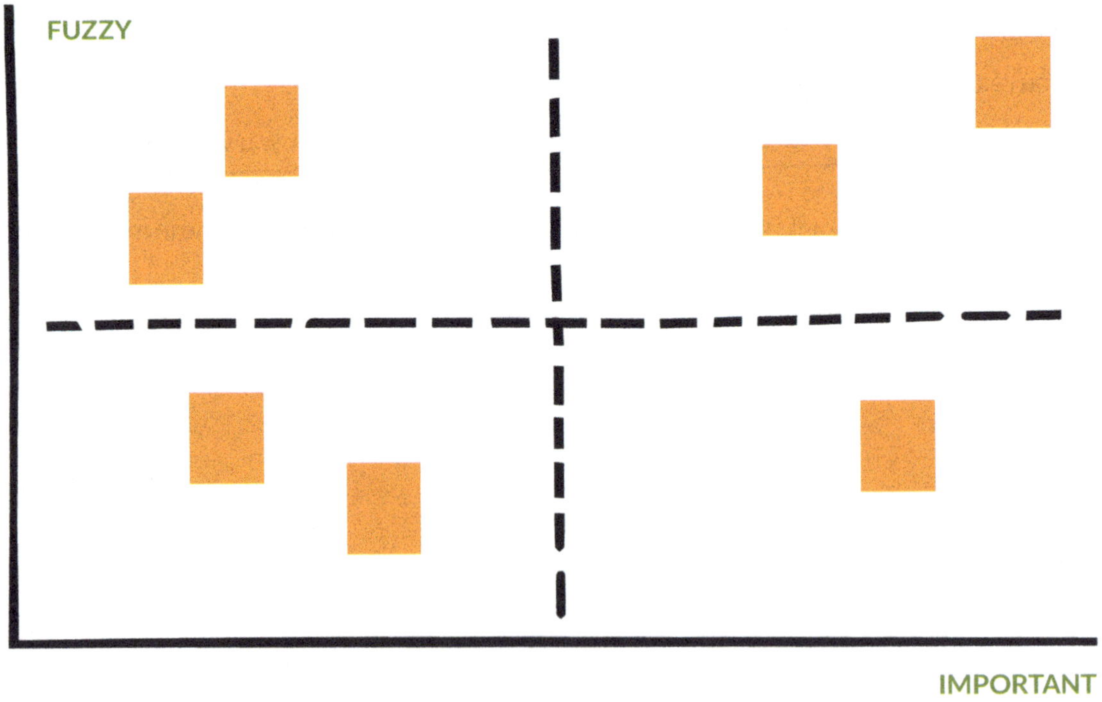

DOWNLOAD

Download the chart.

7.7 NETWORKING

To move forward, you'll need information. To get that information, you'll need to talk to people. And to talk to people… you'll need to meet them. That's where networking comes in.

Now, before you roll your eyes at the word *networking*, let's pause. What does it mean to you?

For some, it's exciting—meeting new people, sharing ideas, making connections. For others, it feels like being dropped into a shark tank with a sticky name tag. Be honest with yourself: do you find it energizing, awkward, context-dependent? There's no wrong answer.

The truth is, you're already part of many networks—friends, neighbors, colleagues, family. You've been building them naturally your whole life. This chapter is about leaning into that, on purpose.

MINDSET

The best networking mindset? Curiosity + generosity.

If you walk in only thinking "what can I get," people will feel it immediately. Instead, focus on genuine interest—listen, ask questions, share openly. Networks thrive on trust, and trust grows when people feel seen and valued. Give as much as you take. Or more.

GOAL

In the context of your Adventure, your goal isn't to collect business cards or LinkedIn connections—it's to gather stories, insights, experiences, and introductions.

And here's the thing: don't force it. Don't ambush strangers with questions like an interrogator at a trade conference. People love to be helpful when they feel respected. They love being recognized for what they know. But they hate being used.

So your goal is simple: *learn with curiosity, connect with respect.*

STRATEGY

Start small. Who already has the information or experience you're looking for? Maybe they're already in your circle. Maybe you need to take one step beyond.

Grab a sheet of paper and do this:

- Write down three people you'd love to talk to about your plan. These can be people you know—or people you want to know.
- Then, write down three ways you could bring value back to your network. Maybe you introduce two people who should meet, share a resource, or simply offer your time.

That's it. Networking shouldn't be transactional—it's planting seeds. Some grow right away, others later. But they only grow if you put them in the ground.

Now go out there—connect, ask, listen, share.

7.8 INTERVIEW SKILLS

Talking to people who've already walked the path you're curious about can be a game-changer. They have the lived experience you don't—yet. The funny thing is, they probably won't even think of it as an interview. To them, it's just a chat over coffee. But for you, it's gold.

That means you need to show up prepared. You're not there for chit-chat. You have a purpose.

And just to be clear:

- You're not asking for advice on what you should do. That's what your dad is for.
- You're not looking for validation, someone to say "Great idea!" That's what your mom is for.

STANDPOINT

The key is this: ask about experiences, not opinions.

Skip the "what do you think" questions. Instead, dive into "what actually happened." Get them to relive their days:

- "What does a typical day look like?"
- "What did you do yesterday?"
- "What's the most boring or frustrating part of your work?"
- "What's the most fun?"
- "What's been your toughest challenge?"

It's like guiding them to close their eyes and replay the movie of their life. Opinions are filtered. Stories are raw.

And when they show emotion—when their face lights up or darkens—that's your cue. Follow that thread. That's where the real insights live.

Be honest with them and yourself. Tell them you want brutal honesty, no sugarcoating. And then, really listen. Let silence do its work—sometimes a pause pulls out the most interesting details.

Yes, you love your idea. Yes, part of you just wants to hear "go for it." Resist. You're not fishing for compliments. You're hunting for reality. And sometimes reality bites—you may hear things that make you doubt your plan. That's okay. It's better to know now than five years down the road.

And remember: one person's story isn't *the truth*. It's just one piece of the puzzle. Talk to several people, gather different perspectives, and then—only then—decide what to do with it.

YOUR TURN

So, go find them. Network. Connect. Talk to the manager of that coffee shop you dream about running. Or the person in that department you want to join.

You'll be surprised at how generous people can be—and how much you'll learn, often from the smallest, most offhand comment.

7.9 CONVERSATION TRACKER

Here's the thing: your brain is a leaky bucket. A week later, even a day later, the golden nuggets from that amazing conversation will have slipped through the cracks. At least that's how it works for me. We always think, *"Oh, I'll remember this—how could I forget?"* And then... we do.

So—don't wait. Write it down.

Right after an interview, block off a little time to capture what you learned. Not just the facts, but also the feelings: what surprised you, what made you pause, what sounded contradictory.

How you track it is up to you. Some people love mind maps—fast, visual, full of connections. Others prefer the neatness of a Word doc or a spreadsheet, each insight on a new line. Whatever works—just do it. Your future self will thank you.

Then, step back and look for patterns.

- Do you keep hearing the same advice over and over? That's a strong signal.
- Did someone share a one-off weird story? Interesting, but maybe an outlier.

The point is to collect, organize, and notice. Each conversation is a puzzle piece. The more you track, the clearer the big picture becomes.

CONVERSATION TRACKER WORKSHEET

Use this table to capture and organize the wisdom you gather from your conversations. Keep it light, keep it clear, and most importantly—don't forget to do it right after the chat!

WHO I TALKED TO	WHEN & WHERE	KEY INSIGHTS	SURPRISES / EMOTIONS	PATTERNS OR CONTRADICTIONS	NEXT STEPS
Coffee shop manager	Mon, Feb 5 – Café Aroma	Running a café is 80% logistics, 20% coffee love.	Surprised: he spends more time with suppliers than with customers.	Matches what another café owner said last week.	Shadow him for a day next month.
HR Director, Tech Co.	Zoom – Feb 7	Promotion = more admin, less creative work.	She laughed about "drowning in Excel sheets."	Contradicts what my colleague told me about her role.	Ask another HR manager for perspective.

Tips for using this tracker:

- Don't just write *what they said—capture how it felt* when they said it.
- Look for repeated themes: if three people say the same thing, pay attention.
- Track your next steps so conversations lead to action, not just notes.

7.10 WRAP UP

Role-play your future. That's what this chapter has really been about—stepping into the shoes of your future self and testing what life could feel like. An interview, a conversation, even a simple observation won't be the same as living it, but it's already a powerful sneak peek.

By now, you've mapped out the key players in your project and practiced telling your story in a way that connects with them. You've spotted the assumptions that could make or break your plan and learned how to test them. You've prepared yourself to network with curiosity and generosity, and you know how to ask the kinds of questions that reveal the real picture.

Now it's time to get out there. Start the conversations. Follow the threads. Gather insights. Each step will give you more clarity, more confidence, and maybe even some surprises.

Go live a slice of your future—today.

08

How do you know if you should jump?

Big decisions can feel overwhelming
Here you'll stress-test your plans with practical tools: mapping enthusiasm and confidence, spotting biases in decision-making, and adopting an agile mindset.

So—you've dreamed, mapped, and even role-played your possible futures. You've got sketches of what your life could look like. But now comes the big question: **Do you actually leap?**

This part is about testing the waters before cannonballing into the pool. You're going to slow down just enough to check: *Is this really for me? Am I excited enough? Confident enough? Or am I chasing an illusion?*

We'll start with an **Evaluation Matrix** to score your ideas—nothing scary, just a way to balance excitement with realism. Then we'll peek into the sneaky **decision biases** that mess with your judgment (spoiler: your brain likes shortcuts, and they're not always helpful).

And finally, we'll borrow from the world of software developers and entrepreneurs: the **agile mindset**. Instead of carving your future in stone, you'll treat it as an experiment. Small steps, quick feedback, and plenty of course corrections.

By the end, you won't just have a plan. You'll have a decision-making process, a safety net, and a way to move forward with confidence. Whether your answer is *"Yes, let's do this!"* or *"Not yet, but I'm learning,"* you'll know exactly where you stand.

8.1 WHAT YOU ARE GOING TO DO

Now comes the fun (and sometimes uncomfortable) part: putting your ideas to the test. We'll walk through a series of tools and mindsets that will help you see if your plan really holds up in the real world.

ATTRACTIVENESS MAP

First, you'll map your enthusiasm and confidence. Step by step, milestone by milestone, you'll ask yourself: *Do I actually feel excited about this?* and *Do I believe I can really pull it off?* Sometimes you'll find high excitement but low confidence—or the other way around. Both matter.

DECISION-MAKING PROCESS

Then we'll revisit your psychological profile from earlier and connect it to the way you usually make decisions. Everyone has blind spots—some people jump in too fast, others get paralyzed by analysis. This part is about spotting your patterns and learning how to work around them so your choices are clearer and wiser.

AGILITY

Finally, a little mindset shift. If this book sometimes sounded like a neat A-to-Z plan, let's be clear: real life isn't that tidy. You'll take wrong turns, backtrack, and reimagine pieces along the way. That's not failure—it's agility. When you treat your plan like an experiment, every stumble is just more data helping you get it right.

8.2 ATTRACTIVENESS TEST

Think of this as a **reality check with a dash of fun**—a way to see which parts of your Adventure light you up and which might secretly drag you down. It's not about judging yourself; it's about mapping out your energy and confidence so you can steer your adventure wisely.

Here's the big question:

- **How excited are you to actually do this thing?**
- **And how confident are you that you can pull it off?**

ENTHUSIASM: THE FUEL

Enthusiasm is your excitement meter. It's the thrill of saying, *"Yes, I can't wait to dive into this!"* Maybe it's because the step feels fun, creative, important, lucrative, impactful—or all of the above. Whatever the reason, your gut says *let's go!*

CONFIDENCE: THE ENGINE

Enthusiasm is great, but you also need the horsepower to move forward. Confidence is about whether you believe you can actually deliver. Can you land the client? Pass the certification? Pitch to investors? Different milestones require different muscles—so which ones do you already have, and which need strengthening?

THE ATTRACTIVENESS MAP

Now the magic tool: a simple chart with two axes:

- **Enthusiasm (1–10)**
- **Confidence (1–10)**

Plotting each step of your plan on this graph is like drawing a treasure map of your future.

This exercise is similar to the "Riskiest Assumptions" one from **Chapter 7.6**, but instead of spotting fuzzy unknowns, you're rating your **energy vs. ability**.

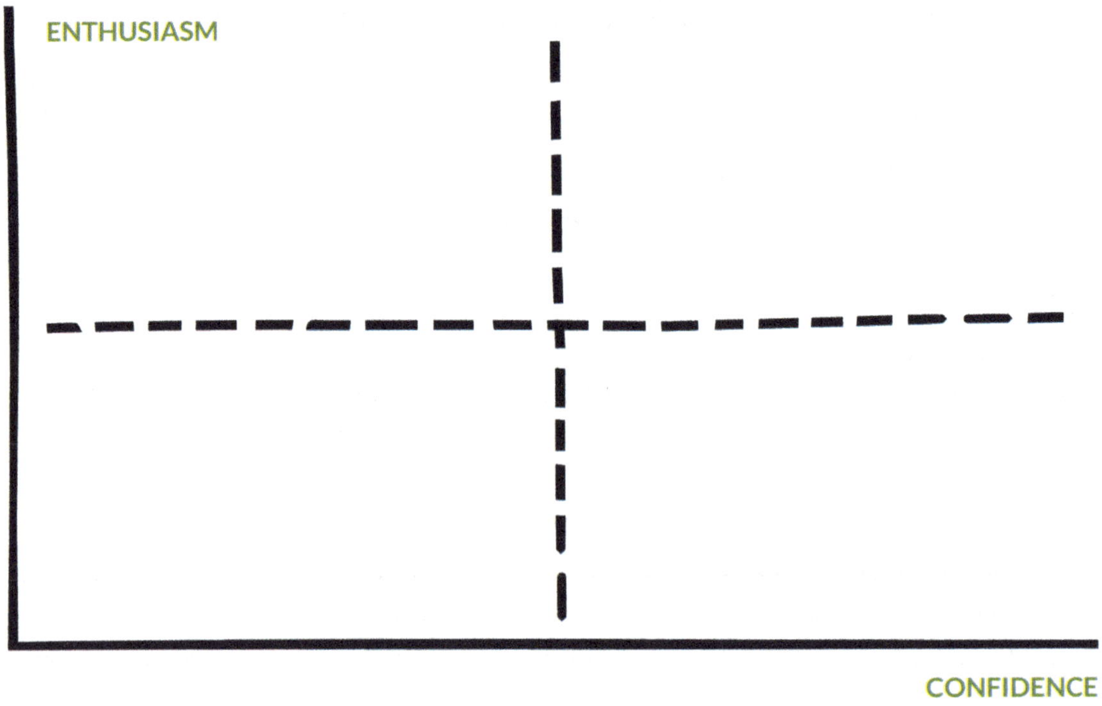

HOW TO PLAY

1. Take your Adventure and list the main steps.
2. For each one, give yourself two scores (1–10): enthusiasm and confidence.
3. Plot them on the graph.

Pro tip: Go big! Use a whiteboard or poster-sized paper and sticky notes. Even better, invite a few trusted friends to play along and challenge your assumptions.

WHAT THE MAP REVEALS

- **Top right corner = gold mine.** High enthusiasm + high confidence = your natural sweet spot.
- **Low enthusiasm zones** (bottom right). If too much of your plan falls here, beware: the day-to-day might drain you more than you think.
- **Low confidence zones** (top left). Ambition is great, but too many items here might mean unnecessary risk. Maybe you need training, partners, or a backup plan.
- **Bottom left = danger zone**. Low excitement and low confidence? That's the quicksand.

WHY IT MATTERS

This exercise forces you to look at every step, not just the fun shiny parts. It highlights blind spots you might otherwise ignore and helps you see where you need support, tweaks, or a rethink.

It's not about killing your dream—it's about making sure your rocket is ready for launch before you press the big red button 🚀.

EXAMPLE

Let's bring this to life with five sample steps. Imagine you're mapping your own plan—it might look a little like this:

1. **Finish your certification as a practitioner**

You're almost there. Honestly? It's kind of dull at this point, but you know you'll get it done.

✨ Enthusiasm = 4 | 💪 Confidence = 9

2. **Find a workspace that fits**

Right size, right location, right price. You've already scouted a few options and the thought of moving into your own space makes you smile.

✨ Enthusiasm = 8 | 💪 Confidence = 8

3. **Recruit a multilingual assistant/receptionist**

This one makes you nervous. What if the chemistry isn't right? What if the market is too tight to find the right fit?

✨ Enthusiasm = 3 | 💪 Confidence = 3

4. **Create a website that actually sells**

Marketing isn't your zone of genius, but you know it's key. Luckily, you've got friends in the field who've offered to lend a hand.

✨ Enthusiasm = 5 | 💪 Confidence = 7

5. **Find your very first customers**

Now this excites you. You love meeting people and you've got plenty of ideas for channels to try. The only catch? You've never actually done it before.

✨ Enthusiasm = 9 | 💪 Confidence = 4

Once you've scored each step, **plot them on the graph**. Suddenly, you'll see your project take shape: the easy wins, the danger zones, and the exciting-but-risky leaps.

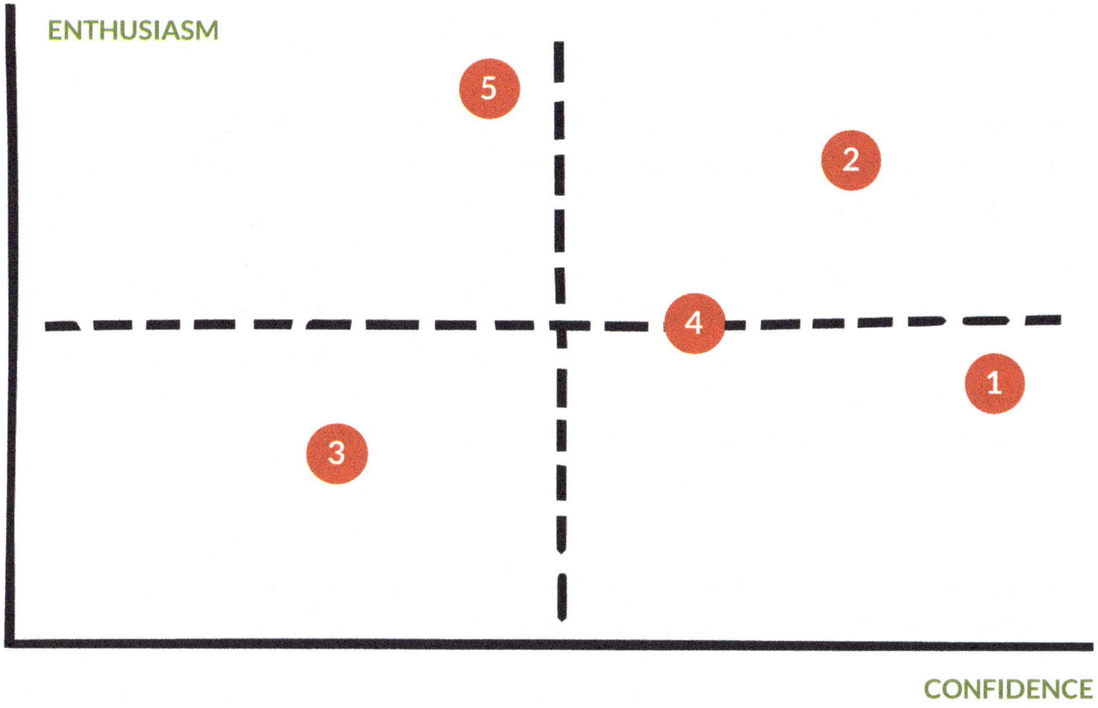

Let's read the map together:

- **#3, hiring an assistant/receptionist, stands out as the weakest spot.** You're dragging your feet, your confidence is shaky, and honestly, you're dreading it. That's a double red flag. But instead of panicking, think options: Could you test the waters with a temp? Share the load with a partner? Or maybe DIY it for a while until you're more comfortable? The key is to find a way to pull that dot up and to the right.

- **#1, finishing your diploma, shows a small enthusiasm dip.** It's not thrilling, but you're already well on your way. This is more of a "grind it out" step than a real problem. Keep pushing through—you've got this.

- **#5, finding your first customers, is the interesting one.** Your enthusiasm is sky-high (yay!), but your confidence lags behind. That imbalance is worth addressing. Could you boost your skills with a short sales course, binge some online resources, or just get out there and practice until it feels natural? Every rep will move that dot closer to confidence.

- And finally, **look at those steps in the magical top-right corner.** High enthusiasm and high confidence—that's your sweet spot. Those are the pieces that will fuel you and keep momentum strong. Give yourself credit for them.

Now, step back. What's the overall picture? Which dots energize you, and which ones drag you down? Most importantly: **does the map still make you excited to move forward with your project?**

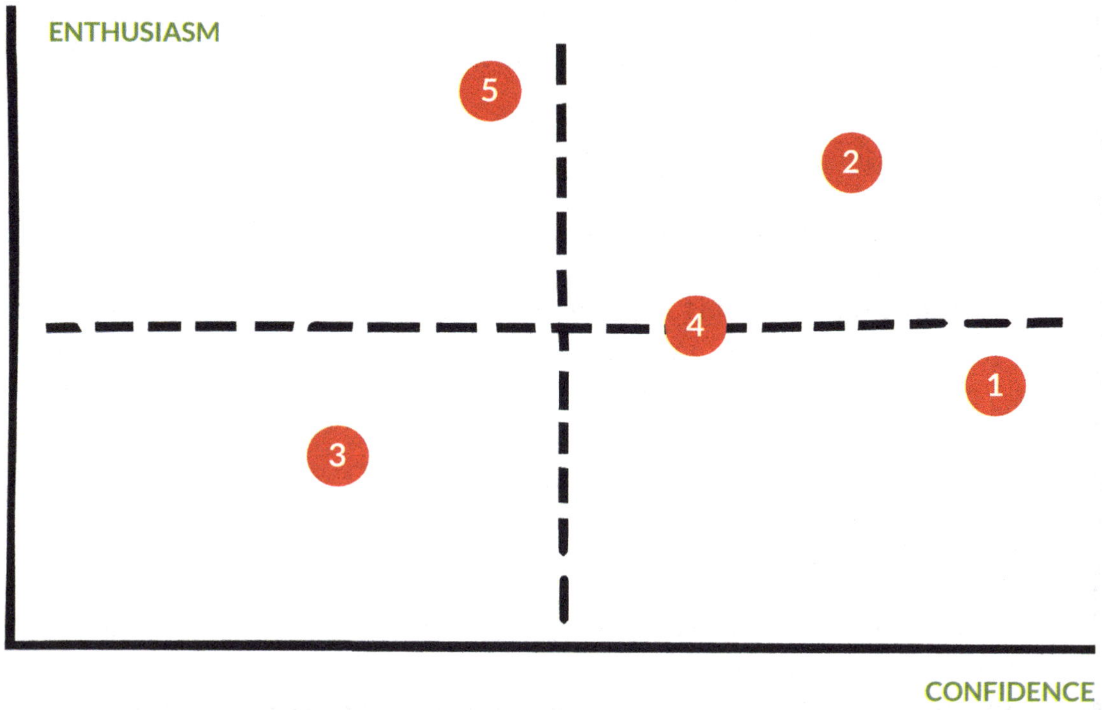
ENTHUSIASM
5
2
4
1
3
CONFIDENCE

Alex

1. **Year One: Family Vacation**

Before the kids leave for university, we'll take an incredible family trip together. I've been the planner of our vacations for years, and I know how to make this unforgettable. I can already picture the laughter, the little adventures, the memories we'll treasure.

✨ Enthusiasm = 10 | 💪 Confidence = 10

2. **Year One: Researching Options**

I'll start exploring what already exists for children in difficult situations—centers, programs, professionals, resources. I'm eager to dig in, like a detective uncovering possibilities. Of course, I might not always like what I find, but I feel ready to face reality.

✨ Enthusiasm = 8 | 💪 Confidence = 8

3. **Year Two: Back to School**

Time to finish my psychology studies. I love the subject, and I know it will give me the tools I need. Still, I can't ignore my nerves—most students will be much younger, and it's been years since I sat in a classroom. But deep down, I trust myself to rise to the challenge.

✨ Enthusiasm = 5 | 💪 Confidence = 8

4. **Year Two: Networking & Vision Building**

I'll begin connecting with people who share this mission and gather their insights to shape my plan, vision, and budget. I thrive on meeting new people—but will I find the right ones, the ones who really "get it"? That uncertainty lingers.

✨ Enthusiasm = 8 | 💪 Confidence = 4

5. **Year Three: Moving & Fundraising**

The kids will have left home, and my partner and I will move into a smaller place. At the same time, I'll focus on building partnerships and raising funds for the center. Honestly? It feels like a lot at once. Exciting, yes, but also stressful. Still, I know I can push through.

✨ Enthusiasm = 3 | 💪 Confidence = 7

6. **Year Four: Opening the Center**

This is the dream becoming real. I can almost feel the energy of the place—the children finding safety, the team working with heart, the sense of purpose. But assembling the right team will be tough, and that uncertainty makes me cautious.

✨ Enthusiasm = 10 | 💪 Confidence = 5

7. **Year Five: Growth & Awareness**

By then, the center is running and growing awareness around this cause. Honestly, it feels like a distant horizon—so many steps stand between here and there. That makes it a little intimidating, almost discouraging. But this is the vision that keeps me going.

✨ Enthusiasm = 4 | 💪 Confidence = 4

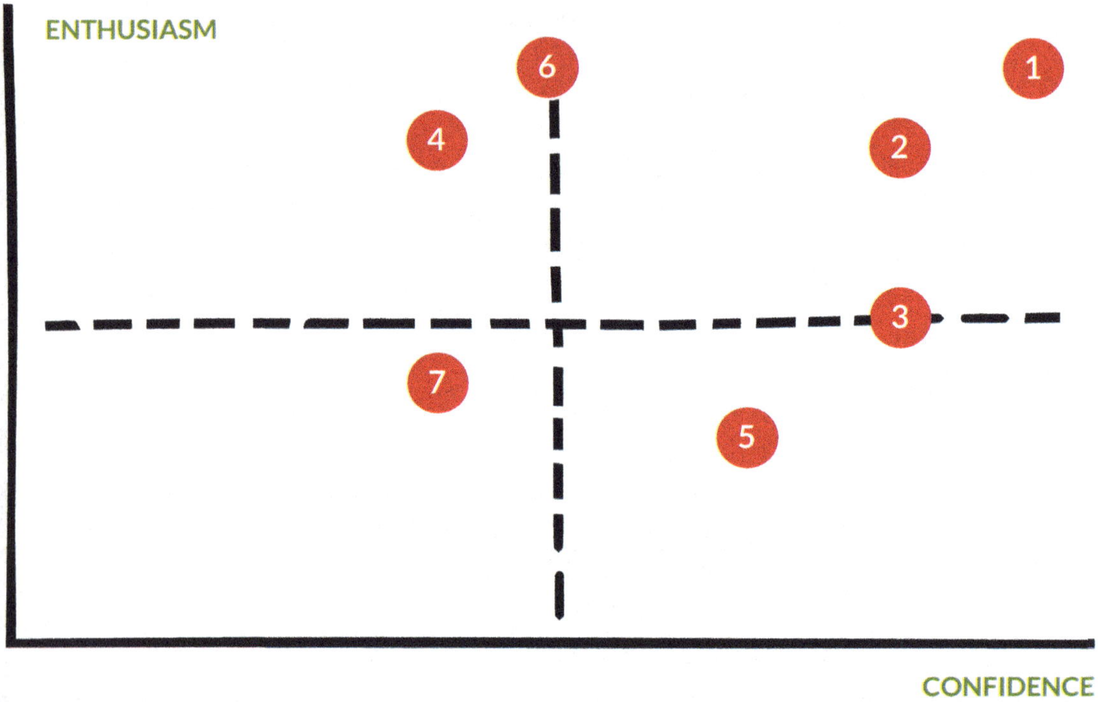
ENTHUSIASM
6
1
4
2
3
7
5
CONFIDENCE

What does this graph show me?

7. I'm excited to begin, but the long-term vision feels overwhelming. Does that mean I need to break it into smaller, more manageable steps?
5. The idea of moving and restructuring my life is scary. Is it too scary, or just the kind of fear that signals growth?
4. My confidence in finding the right people is low. Maybe this is a skill I can build—through practice, training, or even small experiments to test myself.
3. Going back to school will take grit. I know it will stretch me, but also give me what I need to move forward.
6. Building the right team is daunting. I'll need to be intentional—choosing people who not only bring skills, but who share the passion and heart for this work.

How does all this affect my vision?

It shows me where my energy is high, where my doubts live, and where I need to prepare. It doesn't make me want to quit—if anything, it gives me a clearer picture of the hurdles ahead. And that makes the dream feel more real.

Alex

DOWNLOAD

Download the worksheet as a PDF.

REFLECT

So… how did that feel? Eye-opening? A little uncomfortable? Maybe even energizing?

Did the exercise nudge you to look at parts of your plan you were happily ignoring? If yes, what surfaced? Hidden dragons, or just a few cobwebs?

Where did your **enthusiasm dip**? Are those tasks truly dreadful, or just things you haven't figured out how to make more fun yet?

Where did your **confidence waver**? Is it because you really lack the skill, or just because you haven't tested yourself in that area yet?

Most importantly: when you step back and look at the whole picture, does your project feel more solid… or shakier than before?

This reflection isn't about judging yourself — it's about seeing clearly where you shine, and where you'll need backup, practice, or a creative workaround.

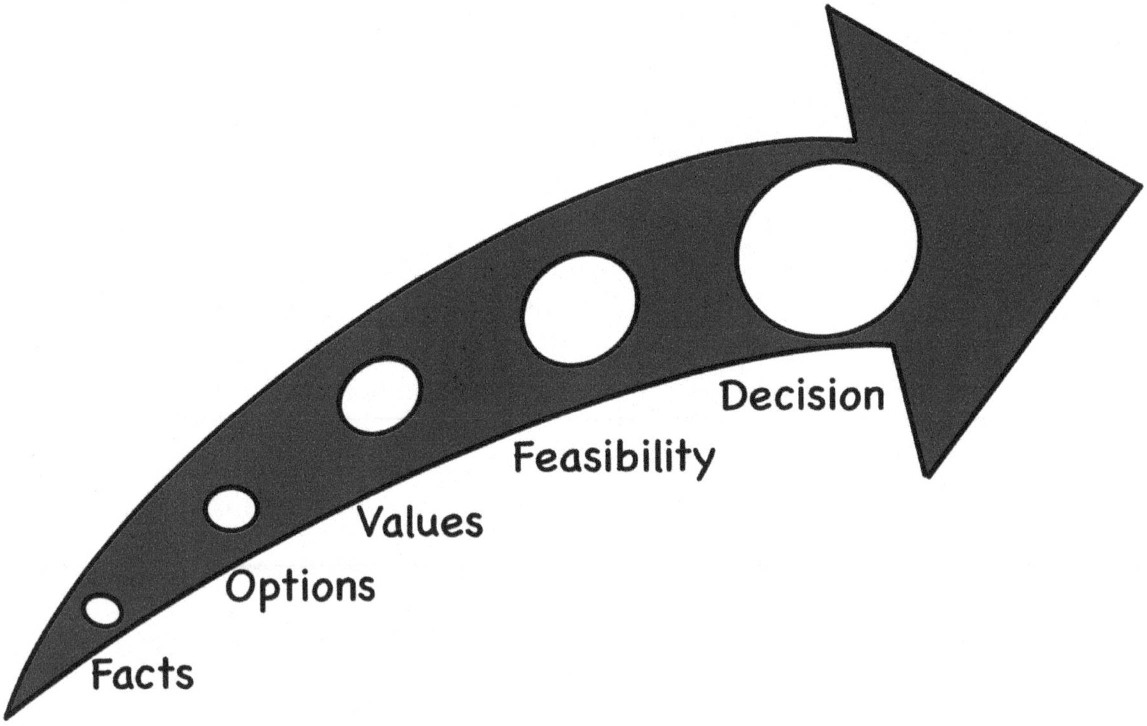
Facts
Options
Values
Feasibility
Decision

8.3 DECISION-MAKING

We all have our own "default mode" when it comes to making decisions. Maybe you go with your gut. Maybe you over-research until your head spins. Maybe you ask three friends and then flip a coin. Whatever your style, it's gotten you this far — but that doesn't mean it's always the best way.

The truth is, we all carry **blind spots, shortcuts, and habits** that quietly shape our choices. Sometimes they help, sometimes they trip us up. With a little reflection — and a bit of structure — we can sharpen the way we decide.

That's the point of this exercise: to step back, see how you usually make decisions, and experiment with a simple but powerful model that can make your process clearer and stronger.

On the left page, you can see the model in a nutshell.

Once we have defined the issue, we can take four steps leading up to the actual decision.

1. **Facts** – First, ground yourself. Gather the data, observe what's really happening, and look at the context. What's true, not just what you assume?

2. **Options** – Next, brainstorm possibilities. Don't stop at the obvious one. (Remember Reframing from **Chapter 5.4**? This is where it pays off!)

3. **Values** – Then, hold those options up to your compass. Do they fit your work view, your life view, your sense of what really matters? (See **Chapter 4.4** if you need a refresher.)

4. **Feasibility** – Finally, test reality. Can this option actually work? What would it take? How hard would it be to pull off?

Only after walking through those steps, do you land on the decision itself.

On paper, it sounds simple. In real life… do we actually go through all four steps? Or do we sometimes skip straight from "gut feeling" to "done deal"?

EXPLORER'S PROFILE

Remember back in **Chapter 4.3**, when you took that personality test? (If not, now's a good time to flip back — we'll wait.) That test explored several traits: Mind, Energy, Nature, Tactics, and Identity.

For decision-making, we're going to zoom in on just two of them: **Energy** and **Nature**.

- **Energy** is about how you see the world and process information.
  - **Observant** types are practical, pragmatic, grounded in the here-and-now.
  - **Intuitive** types are curious, open-minded, and love to imagine what could be.

- **Nature** is about how you make decisions and handle emotions.
  - **Thinking** types rely on objectivity, logic, and analysis.
  - **Feeling** types lead with empathy, values, and emotional connection.

Now, go back to your results. Where did you land on these two scales? And how might that shape the way you make decisions?

(Of course, these are broad generalizations, not absolute truths. But they're useful lenses — and they can teach us a lot about our habits.)

Here's how they link to our **four-step decision model** from earlier:

- **Observant** → naturally strong at step 1: *Facts*
- **Intuitive** → lean toward step 2: *Options*
- **Feeling** → tuned into step 3: *Values*
- **Thinking** → comfortable with step 4: *Feasibility*

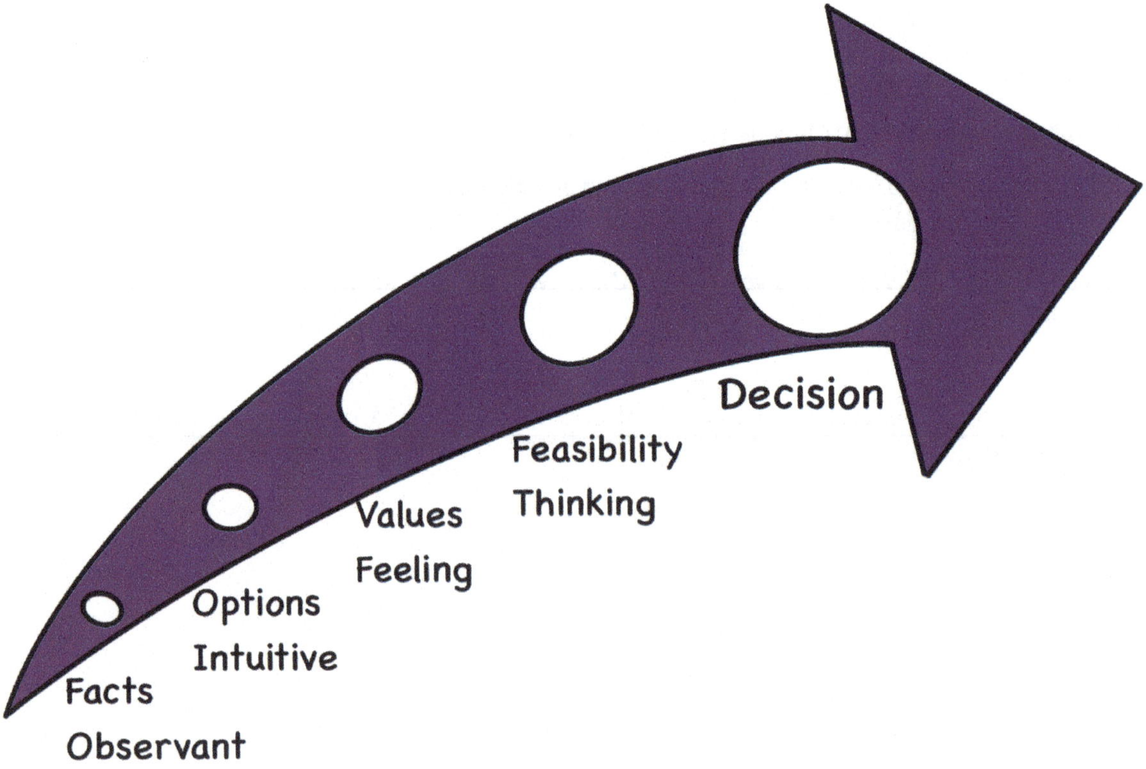

Sounds neat, right? But here's the catch: most of us lean heavily on just *two* of these steps, skipping the others. That turns a rich four-step process into a shortcut two-step process.

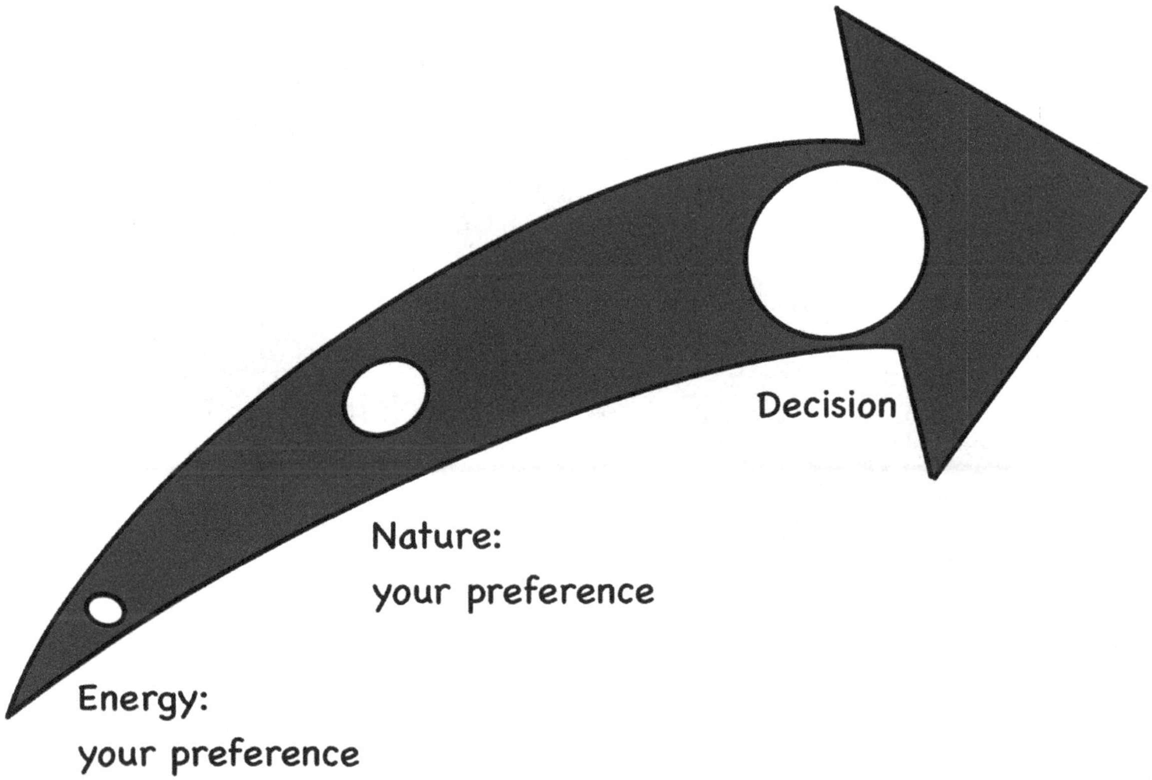

Let's play this out with two opposite examples:

- If you're **Intuitive + Feeling**: you're likely to jump right into exploring *options*, and then filter them through your *values*. If something feels right, boom — decision made. But notice what's missing: you might skip Facts (overlooking crucial info) and *Feasibility* (oops, it turns out your dream solution is wildly impractical).

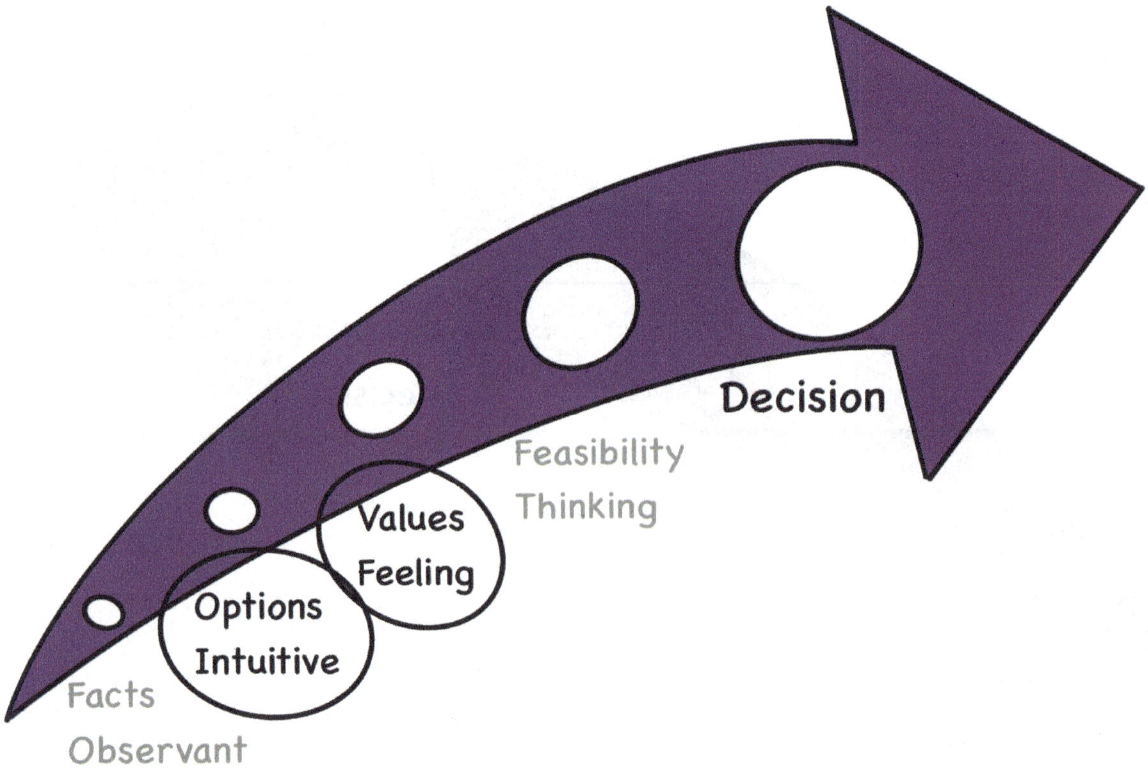

- If you're **Observant + Thinking**: you'll gather *all the data*, then run it through a cool-headed feasibility check. What works? What's efficient? Great — decision done. But what if you've ignored the more creative *options*? Or skipped checking if the decision aligns with your *values*? You might end up with a perfectly rational choice that still feels wrong.

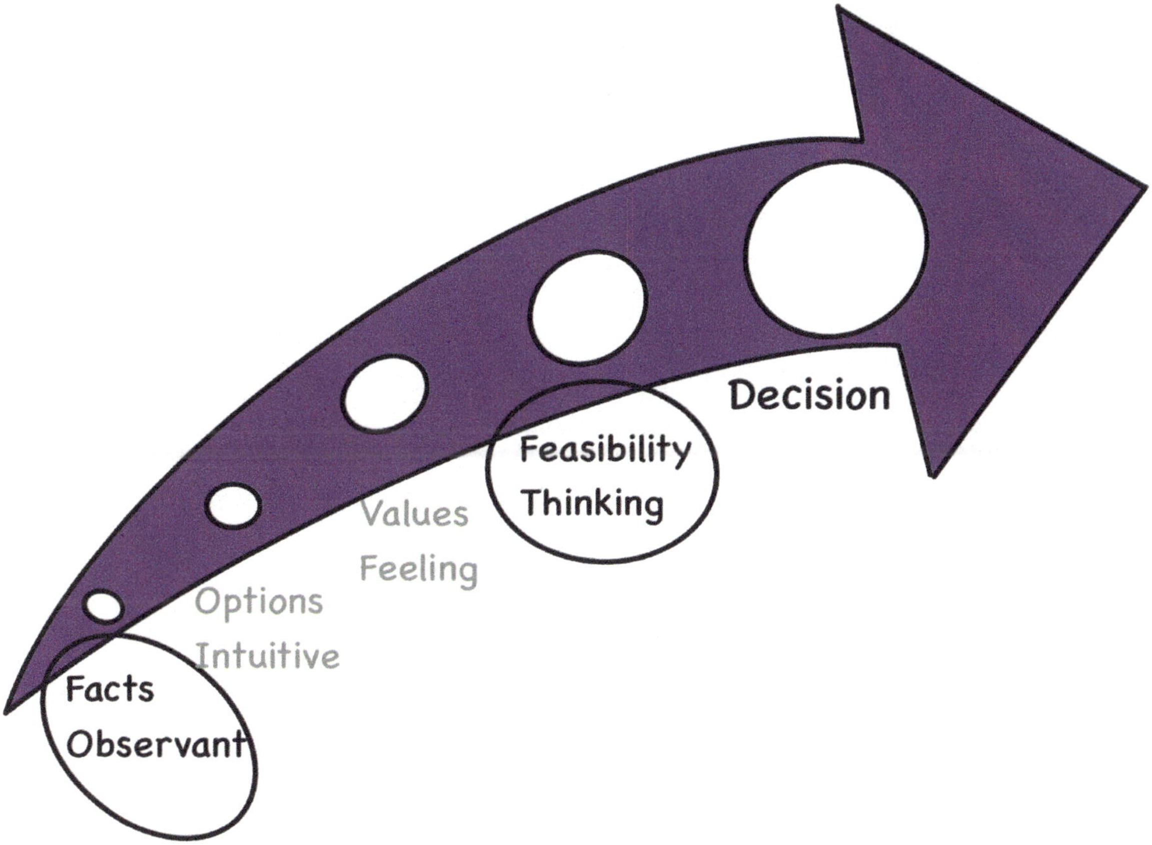

The point isn't to label yourself or fit into a box. Nobody is just one thing — we're all more complex than that. But by recognizing your natural shortcuts, you can **slow down, stretch yourself, and run through all four steps**:

- Gather the facts.
- Explore the options.
- Check what feels right.
- Test what's feasible.

That way, you're not just making faster decisions — you're making *better* ones.

EXERCISE: PUT YOUR DECISION-MAKING UNDER THE MICROSCOPE

Enough theory — let's roll up our sleeves and see how this plays out in real life. Grab the worksheet (or just a notebook), and let's map out how *you* really make decisions.

STEP 1: EXPLORER'S PROFILE

Dig out your 16personalities results (from **Chapter 4.3**). Focus on two traits:

- **Energy:** Observant (S) or Intuitive (N)?
- **Nature:** Thinking (T) or Feeling (F)?

Mark your spot on these spectrums — that's your starting point.

STEP 2: CHECK YOUR NATURAL DECISION MODEL

Now, drop those traits onto the **decision model**. Do you naturally lean toward Facts, Options, Values, or Feasibility? Highlight your "home zones" — the steps where you feel at ease.

STEP 3: SPOT YOUR BLIND SPOTS

This is where it gets interesting. Where do you usually *skip ahead* or rush through? Use the grid to pinpoint areas where you could improve. (Hint: if one or two steps always feel uncomfortable… those are the ones to watch!)

STEP 4: TWEAK YOUR APPROACH

Big changes aren't necessary — even tiny adjustments can shift your whole process. What could you try differently next time you face a decision? Maybe it's slowing down to check the facts, or forcing yourself to consider options outside your comfort zone.

Write down a few ideas. Think of them as "decision experiments" you'll run on yourself.

FACTS-OBSERVANT I gather all the relevant information (facts) without judgement.	☐ Good ☐ Need improvement

OPTIONS-INTUITIVE I can easily imagine different alternatives. I rarely chose the first option that comes to my mind.	☐ Good ☐ Need improvement

VALUES-FEELING I take my values into consideration, and I naturally align my choice with them.	☐ Good ☐ Need improvement

FEASIBILITY-THINKING I can easily imagine how to implement the choice, what are the steps to execute and how to measure the success of the chosen option.	☐ Good ☐ Need improvement

DOWNLOAD

Grab the worksheet as a PDF to guide you.

REFLECT

- Did you spot your personal shortcuts or biases?
- Which step do you tend to overuse… and which ones do you skip?
- How could a small tweak improve the way you decide?

Wow — this model hits home. Every time I make a decision and someone challenges me, I realize I've skipped over the facts and ignored the "how." I get excited about possibilities, but I don't always ground them in reality.

What I need to do is slow down and collect more data before jumping to options:

- What do I actually know?
- What have I observed?
- Where does this information come from?

And once I choose a path, I need to push myself to ask: What's the very next step? What's the concrete, specific action that moves this forward?

To remind myself, I even stuck a little doodle of the model on my fridge 🙂 — so every time I grab a snack, I also grab the thought: "Check the facts, plan the how."

(Alex's profile: Intuitive – Feeling)

Alex

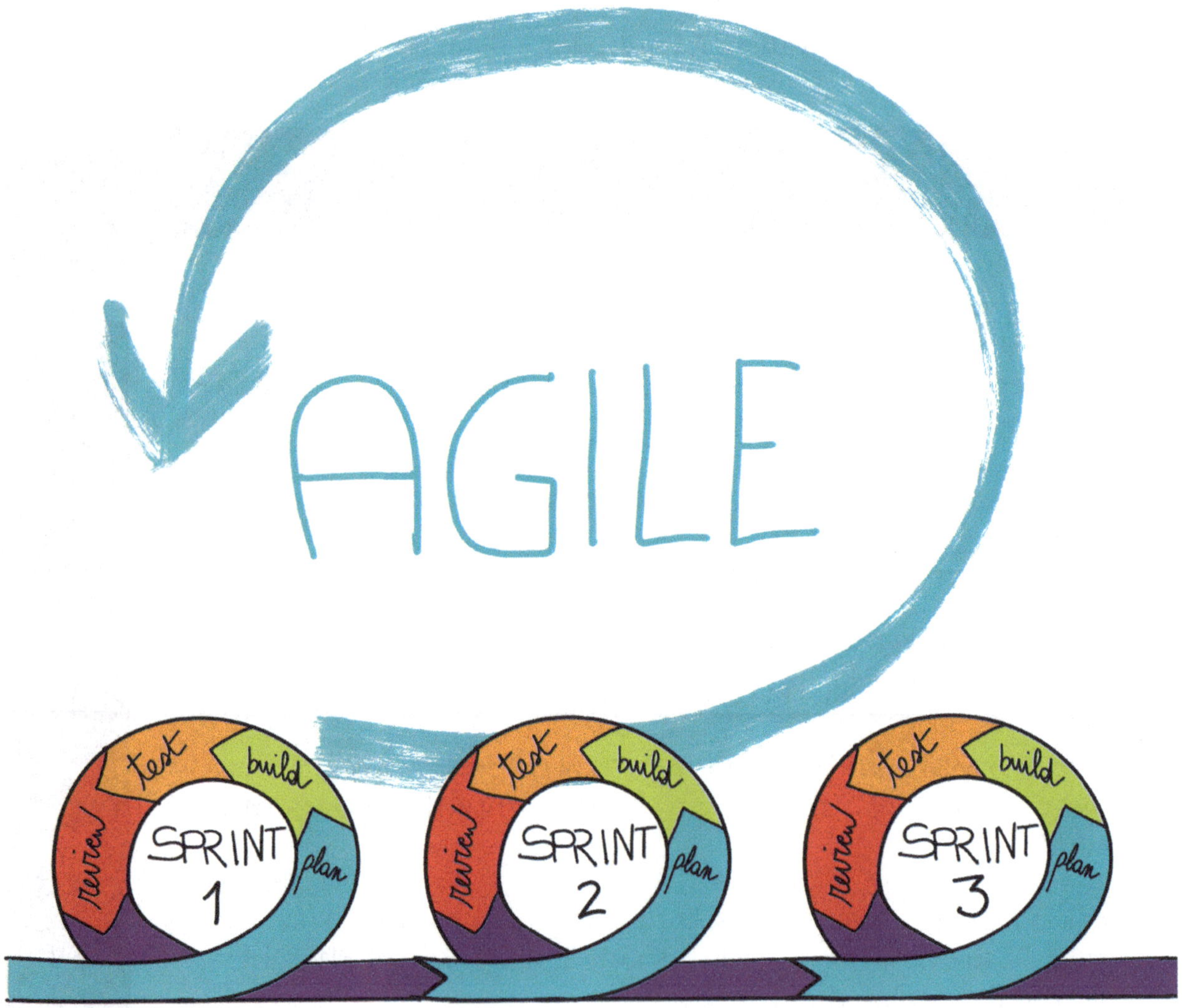
AGILE
test
build
review
SPRINT 1
plan
test
build
review
SPRINT 2
plan
test
build
review
SPRINT 3
plan

8.4 AGILE MINDSET

We live in what experts like to call a **VUCA world**: Volatile, Uncertain, Complex, and Ambiguous. Translation? Things change fast, unpredictably, and often in confusing ways. That makes it much harder to clearly understand what's happening, predict what's coming next, or confidently make decisions.

The truth is, those simple long-term plans—the kind where you map out a straight path and stick to it for decades—don't survive in this kind of world. Life will throw curveballs. Plans will need to bend, flex, sometimes even snap.

So what do we need instead? A different approach—one that keeps us nimble, adaptable, and resilient.

A QUICK TRIP TO THE BUSINESS WORLD

Imagine you're working at a software company a few decades ago. Back then, you could dream up a shiny new product, sketch out a plan, disappear into the office for three years of hard work, and then finally release it. It wasn't risk-free, but the world was stable enough that this worked.

Fast-forward to today. The market moves at lightning speed. Three years is an eternity. By the time you finish, a competitor might have already launched a similar product, customer needs may have shifted, or—let's be real—an unexpected global event could change everything.

Enter **Agile**.

Agile flips the old model on its head. Instead of making one massive plan and locking yourself away until it's "perfect," Agile is about iteration. Build something small, test it, get feedback, adapt. Then repeat. Over and over.

Think of it like climbing a mountain: instead of plotting the whole route from the base to the summit and hoping the weather doesn't change, you climb step by step, pausing to check conditions, adjust your path, and keep moving forward.

In the old way, all the big decisions happened up front—you set the train in motion and just hoped the tracks were still there at the end. Too often, they weren't.

In the Agile way, decisions (and risks) are spread across the journey. Plan, build, test, review, repeat. You're always moving, but always adjusting.

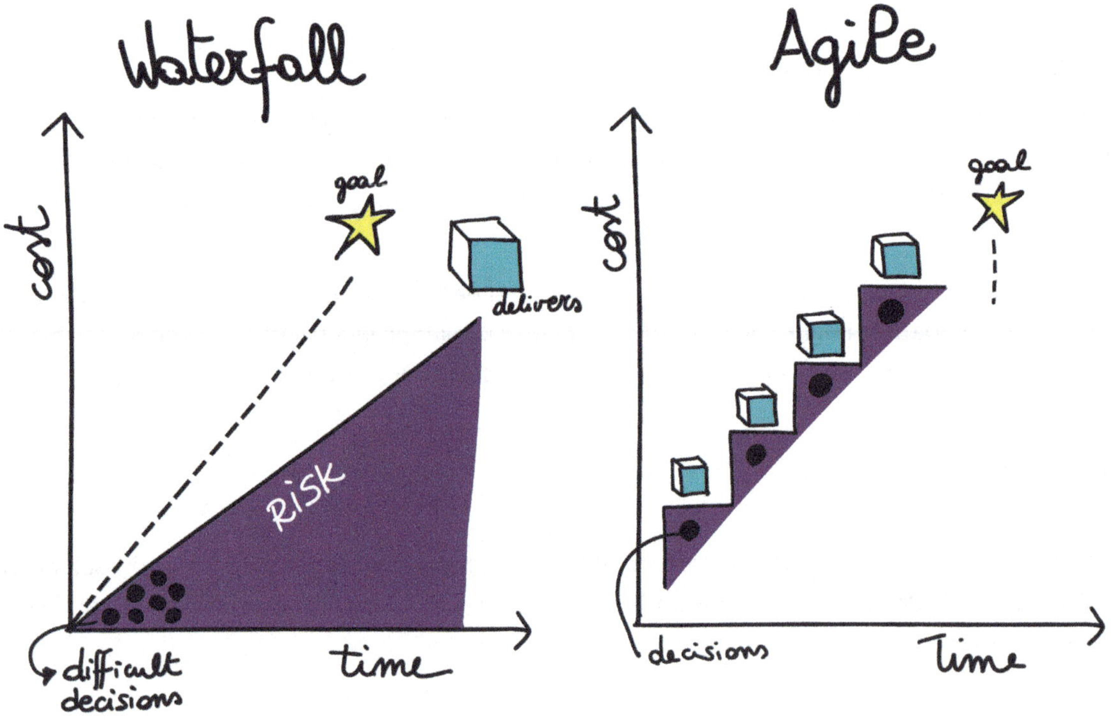

WHAT DOES THIS HAVE TO DO WITH YOU?!?

Once upon a time, a career looked like a straight railway track. Our parents (or grandparents) often stepped onto it at the beginning and rode it all the way to retirement: start as an accountant, finish as an accountant, often in the *same company.*

That world doesn't exist anymore.

Today, things shift fast. Companies rise and fall, entire industries change shape, technology flips the rules overnight. The "straight line" career has turned into more of a winding hiking trail—you can't always see around the bend, and the terrain keeps changing.

So what do you do? You get *agile.*

Instead of "school, then work, then retirement," we need to embrace lifelong learning. Instead of sticking to a single profession, we'll probably move across jobs, companies—even industries. That's normal now.

The trick is to **iterate your way forward**: take a step, get feedback, see how it feels, adjust your plan, and step again. You can absolutely have a long-term dream, but the plan to get there? That has to stay flexible.

MINDSET

Remember when the big measure of success was IQ? Then came EQ (emotional intelligence). Now it's AQ—**Adaptability Quotient**. In other words, how well you roll with the punches.

Adopting an agile mindset means shifting how you see yourself and your journey.

- **The path is more important than the goal.**
  We often tell ourselves, "Once I achieve X, then I'll finally be happy." That's dangerous. If you don't get X, you feel like a failure. If you do get X—then what? Cue existential crisis. Research shows we're happier not from a one-time "win," but from continuously doing interesting, meaningful things along the way. Agile keeps you curious and engaged on the path, not just chasing the finish line.

- **There is no failure.**
  In the old model, if your big plan derails—wrong job, wrong company, wrong timing—it's a *failure*. With Agile, there's no such thing. You try, you learn, you adapt. "Failure" is proof you're pushing boundaries and stepping outside your comfort zone. If you never "fail," chances are you're not growing—you're just coasting.

- **There is no life-or-death decision.**
  Choosing a career path, starting a project, testing a plan—none of these lock you in for life. If it doesn't work, you've gained experience, resilience, and clarity for the next adventure. Agile lowers the stakes and frees you up to explore, play, and experiment.

The Agile mindset turns life into a series of sprints instead of one endless marathon. Short steps, frequent check-ins, constant learning, and—hopefully—a lot more fun.

REFLECT

How does this idea land with you? When you look back at your own life, do you see places where you were already being agile—whether you realized it or not?

How could you bring more agility into the way you make decisions about the future?

And maybe most importantly: what's one small, concrete thing you could try *today* that would move you a little closer to this agile way of living?

Alex

Agile mindset - I need to be agile and still I feel I am coming from the "old waterfall world". My role models (of course my parents, but not only) had the same job, the same house, mainly the same friends for all their lives. And they usually went on holiday to the same places...

Yes, the old "reassuring and stable" world - and yet boring and static.

After my graduation, I remember the idea of imagining my future, making a big plan and then... the big bang delivery...

And I kind of did it. Got my first job in a big multinational company, worked hard to get the first promotion, then the second... got married, had kids, worked hard to be a good parent and changed jobs (new promotions, more money, more opportunities for my family)... a bit of a hamster on the wheel (I admit, it was also comfortable sometimes).

Now I like the idea of the small steps, the doing and learning loops. It is not deciding on one big life plan and then just executing. It is more like aligning to what is important to me all the time.

And by the way, I like the idea of alignment. It is dynamic, active, and, despite bad days, it is always possible to improve.

09

How did you engage with this book?

Everyone comes to this book in their own way. Maybe you raced through it, maybe you tiptoed, maybe you wrestled with every exercise. However you did it—you're here now, which means you're curious about your future. And that's already a win.

So which type of reader are you?

1) YOU JUMPED STRAIGHT TO THE CONCLUSION OUT OF CURIOSITY.

We see you. You wanted the ending first.

Our official advice: buy ten more copies and give them to all your friends.
(Just kidding. Kind of.)

But seriously—circle back, actually *read* the book, and let it change you. You deserve it. We love you too.

2) YOU SKIMMED THROUGH AND NOW FEEL OVERWHELMED.

Take a deep breath. This isn't a test. It's a journey. And journeys are better with company.

Find a **journey buddy**—someone who can listen, challenge, cheer you on, or even do the program alongside you.

And remember: you don't have to do it all at once. Start small. Pick one exercise that feels fun or easy. Before you know it, you'll be hooked—and discovering things about yourself you didn't even know were there.

3) YOU READ IT ALL THE WAY THROUGH AND ARE NOW READY TO ACTUALLY GET TO WORK.

Amazing. You've got the big picture—now it's time to zoom in.

Don't wait too long. Keep that spark alive. Start today, even with something tiny.

Follow the method. It works. You don't need to complete every single exercise, but don't skip the ones that stretch you—those are often where the magic hides.

And whenever you feel lost, loop back. The earlier chapters will always be there to support you.

4) YOU DID EVERY WORD, EVERY EXERCISE, AND STILL DON'T KNOW YOUR NEXT STEP.

First: wow. That's commitment. We're proud of you. Really.

Second: don't give up. This happens more often than you think. Sometimes the dream project looks shinier in your head than on paper. That's normal. That's learning.

Ask yourself:

- Does the project not excite me anymore?
- Does it feel unrealistic—or just too scary?
- Am I solving the *wrong problem*?

If the day-to-day activities bore you, revisit your **Adventure Style (Chapter 4.6)** to reconnect with what energizes you.

If none of your ideas spark joy, head back to **Design Your Adventure (Chapter 6.3)** and dream up wild new options. Go a little crazy this time.

And if you realize you're actually content where you are—that's a win too. Sometimes clarity means seeing that the fantasy wasn't what you really wanted.

5) YOU DID EVERY EXERCISE AND BUILT A WONDERFUL PROJECT FOR THE COMING YEARS.

Bravo. Seriously. You rock.

Now—go live it. But also know this: nothing is locked in. Life will keep evolving, and so will you. Don't be afraid to loop back, re-explore, and redraw your plans. This could be in a year, in ten years, or tomorrow.

There will always be a next chapter in your story. And you're the one writing it.

So—how did you engage with this book? However you did it, thank you for showing up for yourself. That's the first step toward designing a life that feels truly yours.

10 Conclusion

We hope this book has been more than just helpful — we hope it has been a spark. A spark that has opened your eyes to new possibilities, nudged you to experiment, and maybe even shifted the way you think about your life.

Because in the end, this isn't only about designing your *next project.* It's about cultivating a new mindset: one that is more agile, more playful, more compassionate toward yourself. One where you give yourself permission to test, to learn, to adjust, and to find joy along the way.

If you've made it this far, you're already doing it. You're already on the path to a more fulfilling, purposeful life.

EXTRAS

And this isn't the end — it's simply a checkpoint. In the next chapter, you'll find links to a set of resources to keep you going.

So here we are. The final page. But not the final step.

Your next chapter isn't written in here — it's waiting for you, out there.

Go build it. Play with it. Test it. Share it. Live it.

Wow. What a ride. When I first opened this book, I thought I was just going to "figure out my next step." But what I found was so much more.

I've mapped plans, tested assumptions, wrestled with doubts, and even surprised myself with new possibilities. Some parts were uncomfortable (hello, riskiest assumptions!), some were fun (cover story vision!), and others were downright transformative.

The biggest shift? I don't see my future as one big scary leap anymore. I see it as a series of small experiments. I don't have to get it perfect. I just have to keep moving, keep learning, and keep adjusting. That feels... freeing.

Do I know exactly what my life will look like in five years? Nope. But I do know this: I'm not stuck. I'm building. And that makes all the difference.

So here's to the next chapter — messy, exciting, and full of possibility.

Alex

That's it.
Have a great life.

JOHN & LUISA

N
E
O
S

11
Extras

COMPANION WEBSITE

Our companion website contains extra information (that will keep growing).
Go to **ChartingYourRetirementJourney.com.**

WORKSHEETS

All the tools and templates you've used throughout the book, gathered in one place. Use them, reuse them, and make them your own.

EXTRA TOOLS & METHODS

We kept this book focused and practical — not overwhelming. But for those who want more, we've included additional exercises, frameworks, and organizational tools to help you go deeper.

DESIGN THINKING

A short background on the method that inspired this program. In business, it's used to create new products. Here, you've used it to create something even more precious: your life.

BOOKS WE LOVE

A curated list of works that inspired us (and from which we happily "borrowed" ideas). Think of it as your optional extended reading list.

12 The authors

standpoint

◀ LinkedIn

12.1 JOHN ELBING

Storybuilder • Strategy & Marketing coach

I'm passionate about one thing: helping people understand themselves, whether in a professional crossroads or a personal transition, then figure out what comes next with clarity rather than guesswork.

Born in the U.S. and raised in Switzerland, I've zigged and zagged through careers that rarely follow a straight line. I moved from coding to finance, from international organizations to startup life, and eventually into the strange and fascinating world of story and strategy. Each shift added another layer to how I see people, decisions, and the invisible forces that shape our choices. Along the way, I picked up an MS in Computer Science, an MBA in Finance, and certifications in Design Thinking, the StoryBrand framework, and Where to Play.

My work today blends all of that. I coach entrepreneurs, executives, and creatives, not by telling them who they should be, but by helping them read their own map and redesign it when needed. I've launched two startups, supported countless founders through their pivots and breakthroughs, and learned firsthand that life design is not a single moment. It is a series of experiments, reflections, and course corrections that slowly form a coherent direction.

This book gathers the tools, practices, and lessons that have shaped my own path. It's built on years of testing ideas, discarding what doesn't serve, keeping what works, and remembering that reinvention is always possible. I've been designing my life for decades. Now I'm inviting you to build yours, one intentional step at a time.

12.2 LUISA COLOMBO

People & Organizational Developer • Agile HR Practitioner • Coach

InsideOut
People Consulting

LinkedIn ▶

I'm passionate about people—their growth, their interactions, and the invisible mechanics that make collaboration work.

Throughout my career, I've helped organizations, leaders, and teams navigate change and shape environments where people can truly thrive. My background blends economics, human resources, and organizational development, enriched by certifications in coaching and Agile HR practices. I bridge analysis and empathy—mixing data-driven insight with a deeply human approach.

Curious and enthusiastic by nature, I've always seen life as a learning journey. I love exploring new options and asking myself and my clients the same question: "What do you want to grow into next?" That curiosity has guided me across cultures and industries, from corporate HR roles to independent consulting—always with one goal in mind: unlocking human potential.

Over the years, I've coached executives and professionals to design their careers intentionally, develop new capabilities, and bring more meaning and energy into their work and life. I've learned that growth isn't a phase—it's a mindset, a way of engaging with the world.

This book gathers the lessons, stories, and tools that have inspired me most: how to stay curious, experiment with change, and design a life that keeps evolving. I'm still enjoying the process of designing and reshaping my own life—now I'm inviting you to take the next step on yours.

13
Table of contents

TABLE OF CONTENTS

ALEX

DYSFUCTIONAL BELIEFS

14
Sidebars

Flash the QR code

and download all the worksheets.

Made in United States
Orlando, FL
04 November 2026

90206694R00168